PATTY MURPHY

T0286830

zero waste quilting

38 PROJECTS USE EVERY SCRAP WITH STYLE

stashBOOKS
an imprint of C&T Publishing

PUBLISHER: Amy Barrett-Daffin

CREATIVE DIRECTOR: Gailen Runge

SENIOR EDITOR: Roxane Cerda

TECHNICAL EDITOR: Debbie Rodgers

COVER/BOOK DESIGNER: April Mostek

PRODUCTION COORDINATOR: Zinnia Heinzmann

ILLUSTRATOR: Linda Johnson

PHOTOGRAPHY COORDINATOR: Rachel Ackley

FRONT COVER PHOTOGRAPHY by Picture This! Photography

PHOTOGRAPHY by Picture This! Photography, unless otherwise noted

PHOTOGRAPHY on pages 9–16, 62, 66, 76, 78, 84, 90, 96, and 107 by Patty Murphy.

PAPER TEXTURE by Paladin12/Shutterstock.com

FLORAL ILLUSTRATIONS by DesignECShop/Shutterstock.com

Published by Stash Books, an imprint of C&T Publishing, Inc., P.O. Box 1456, Lafayette, CA 94549

Library of Congress Cataloging-in-Publication Data

Names: Murphy, Patricia Priven, 1974- author.

Title: Zero waste quilting : 38 projects use every scrap with style / Patty Murphy.

Description: Lafayette, CA : Stash Books, an imprint of C&T Publishing, [2024] | Summary: "Jump into Zero Waste Quilting! Change the way you quilt and learn how using the fabrics you've purchased and cherished allow you to help sustain the environment and continue making beautiful quilts. Inside quilters will find 38 quilts and small projects that show unique ways to use up small scraps"-- Provided by publisher

Identifiers: LCCN 2024018012 | ISBN 9781644034712 (trade paperback) | ISBN 9781644034729 (ebook)

Subjects: LCSH: Quilting--Patterns. | Patchwork--Patterns. | Waste minimization. | BISAC: CRAFTS & HOBBIES / Quilts & Quilting | CRAFTS & HOBBIES / Sewing

Classification: LCC TT835 .M8478 2024 | DDC 746.46/041--dc23/eng/20240607

LC record available at https://lccn.loc.gov/2024018012

Printed in China

10 9 8 7 6 5 4 3 2 1

Dedication

For Laura, my sister and best friend.

Acknowledgments

Every book features a cast of characters who help an author weave beauty within its pages, and this book is no exception. My eternal gratitude and love to the women who lift me up daily: Amy, Ashley, Beth, Casey, Ginny, Holly, Jill, Sara, and Shelley; the Birds who whisper in my ear, Merry and Jackie; those who share my secrets and keep me laughing, Elizabeth, Kendra, Marnie, Hope and Mary; and old friends Regina and Greg, who helped me bring this book home to Inman Park. Thanks to my parents for graciously agreeing to chauffeur Greg and me all over their beautiful property (and feed us!) so we could capture photos for this book. And most importantly, heartfelt appreciation to my husband, Mike, and our boys. Your unwavering support means everything.

A special thanks to Jennifer for writing the foreword to this book—it's been a privilege to get to know you—and to the industry that supported me with materials for these projects: Quilters Dream Batting, Aurifil Thread, and Andover Fabric. Additionally, my gratitude extends to the editors, artists, and the entire team at C&T Publishing for helping me make this dream a reality, especially Roxane, Debbie, and April.

projects

Metaphor 22

Foreword

by Jennifer Sampou

Zero Waste Quilting by Patty Murphy is a beacon of inspiration for anyone looking to marry their love for quilting with a sincere commitment to sustainability. With 38 ingenious sewing projects, Patty guides us through transforming every scrap of fabric into something beautiful and functional, urging us to see our stash—and our world—with fresh eyes.

I remember meeting Patty at my fabric booth at the Houston Quilt Market in 2019. We became fast friends and bonded over our mutual appreciation for nature and our concerns about the quilting industry's increasing trend toward overconsumption and that too much stuff isn't a good thing. Patty's passion for both gorgeous fabrics and environmental conservation shines through every page, challenging us to rethink our habits and embrace a more intentional approach to making.

Her book is rooted in the principle that creativity flourishes within constraints. By focusing on four main quilt designs and their subsequent projects, Patty proves that nothing needs to go to waste. From the remnants of one project springs the seed for the next, ensuring that even the tiniest pieces find new life. This approach not only challenges the prevailing "buy or die" mentality but also rekindles the original spirit of quilting—a craft born from necessity and ingenuity.

Beyond quilting, Patty's philosophy nudges us towards a more mindful lifestyle across all aspects of our lives, proving that small, everyday choices can indeed lead to significant positive changes. *Zero Waste Quilting* isn't just a collection of projects; it's a heartfelt journey towards sustainability, woven with Patty's personal anecdotes and insights that make it a delight to read.

In essence, this book celebrates the quilt industry's potential for creativity and community while acknowledging its ability to reduce waste. Patty's work is a vibrant reminder that we can pursue our passions in a way that is kinder to our planet. She invites us to join her in taking small steps toward a more sustainable future—one quilt project at a time. Through *Zero Waste Quilting*, Patty doesn't just teach us to quilt with zero waste; she inspires us to live with intention.

Jennifer Sampou

preface

> " A journey of a thousand miles begins with a single step." **ATTRIBUTED TO CHINESE PHILOSOPHER LAO TZU**

Over the last 25 years, I've become increasingly aware of the environmental crisis facing us. What began as thoughtful conversations with my friend Renee about her habits in the late 90s has since inspired change, and while this ethos becomes more and more prevalent in my life, I admit I'm not perfect, nor do I claim to be, 100 percent of the time. However, I know that every small thing I do to honor those concerns is important and I hope that I can inspire change in others. Small habits build upon each other. For me, the two most important habits I continue to try to address are minimizing waste to extend the life cycle of everything and being intentional with purchases. The simple fact is that I don't need everything, and overconsumption is a huge part of the problem we face.

As I've evolved and my concern for our planet and its future has grown, due in no small part to thinking about how my children will manage this problem years from now, I've been forced to look at textiles. I had to look at my stash—my overflowing fabric piles and bins—and I've started to come to terms with what those fabrics mean in the greater global picture.

How much is too much?

I consider myself lucky to be part of an industry that creates such beauty and brings such joy, comfort, and friendship and fellowship to people, but this industry leads us to believe that if we don't buy all the fabric now, we miss out, that we're less than if we don't have a closet full of all the latest popular fabrics. Sure, if we don't buy the new fabric, we do miss out, but what happens when the next line of beautiful fabric comes

out? Do you buy it, too, so you don't miss out? And more importantly, if you do have it, are you using it?

I recognize that to have a thriving quilt industry, we need fabric, thread, patterns, gadgets, and more so we can make our art, but this is where the conversation needs to change. What if we buy with the intent to maximize how we use fabric and tools, and we don't accept waste as the cost of being creative? We can both support the quilting industry and do our part not to litter landfills with excess textiles.

I'll be honest, reconciling how much I love fabric with the knowledge that the process of making fabric is harmful to the planet has not been easy. As an admitted fashion and textile lover since childhood, looking at textiles in any way other than with complete adoration has been a very hard and slow change to make. Over the last few years, I've gone from buying all the fabric to mostly buying fabric when I need something to fill a gap for a project I'm making. I go to my stash a lot and while I do still occasionally purchase small amounts of yardage to fill out a part of my stash again, my mantra has changed significantly.

For some time now, this mindset has carried over into my life in other ways. Once I started to consider how much all my purchases impacted the world around me, I slowly stopped buying as much. Clothes, food, and virtually every aspect of my life has been positively impacted by this decision. Every day I help the environment by actively refusing to give in to overconsumption, and as a bonus, I feel lighter and have less stuff cluttering my space and my mind.

She who dies with the most fabric doesn't win—she leaves a lot of pretty fabric sitting on a shelf.

introduction

> " I think having land and not ruining it is the most beautiful art that anybody could ever want to own." **ANDY WARHOL**

In the know. The world is consuming and producing more material goods than ever before. In fact, according to the United Nations, the global material footprint (raw materials extracted to meet the demand of consumption) has risen from 43 billion metric tons in 1990 to 92 billion in 2017, representing a 113 percent increase.[1] We are using raw materials faster than they can be replenished.

We are producing textiles faster than we can use them, but there are steps we can take to help ameliorate consumption rates. We all know how to reduce, reuse, and repurpose, but we can also refuse and redesign.

As consumers, we can refuse to buy in excess, we can say no to plastic or other packaging, and we can even choose to buy organic textiles. We all have a fabric stash. When you find that next great project, look to your stash first before running out to buy the fabrics shown in the sample.

We can also reduce by design. Traditionally, most of us make a quilt and put the scraps aside. While most of those scraps are *usually eventually* used, what if those scraps aren't used? For this book I changed how I designed the projects by designing with intent. I'll show you how to create quilts and then how to make additional projects until all the fabric is used up. You'll end up with no rogue blocks, no scraps, and virtually no waste.

There was a wonderful secondary phenomenon that happened when I was designing the quilts for this book. When I forced myself to work within a set of constraints—having to use all of the fabric set aside from the main project—I had to get really creative. I had to think about *how* to use the scraps to create something else I loved, and I can unequivocally say that every project created from the quilt leftovers is something I love.

The idea behind this book is layered, yet simple. First, I want you to recognize the power of your stash. Use the fabrics you already own to create the vibrant, dynamic quilts in this book, or any other book or project, with little to no fabric purchased. In fact, apart from backings, I made most of the quilts in this book with fabric from my stash. Second, if you do need or choose to buy yardage or supplement your stash to make a quilt in this book, you can make the secondary projects to still end up with virtually no waste. Regardless of the way you procure fabric, the result is you reduce consumption by using fabric you already own (refusing to buy more), supplementing with small amounts of fabric you need (refusing to buy in excess), and utilizing the material to the end (redesigning). It's an ingenious idea in quilt design and scrap management, and a better use of our resources.

In the know. It is estimated that the textile and garment industry accounts for 1.7 billion tons, or 6–8 percent, of global carbon emissions annually.[2]

> " By discovering nature, you discover yourself." **MAXIME LAGACÉ**

1.unstats.un.org/sdgs/report/2019/goal-12/

2. ilo.org/legacy/english/intserv/working-papers/wp053/index.html

tools needed

Basic quilt-making and sewing supplies are needed to make the projects in this book, but here are a few items that might be particularly helpful in making some of the projects. I recommend you have the following tools to complete the projects in this book.

1/4" Presser Foot

My go-to presser foot is my 1/4" foot. Each side of the foot is 1/4" from the needle. Simply line up the edge of your fabric with the edge of the foot to ensure an accurate seam allowance when you sew. If you don't have a 1/4" presser foot, move your needle to the right or left to correct the seam width. If your needle doesn't move, place a piece of tape across the throat plate to mark where the edge of the fabric should be to get a 1/4" seam allowance. Just be sure not to cover your feed dogs.

Design Wall

A design wall is an invaluable tool in any quilt space. It gives you a place to put your in-progress quilt blocks so you can step back and evaluate your block placement and colors before it's made. To create my design wall, I wrapped a foam insulation board in batting and secured it to the wall using adhesive strips. I like foam insulation because it's light and sturdy, and I can stick pins in it if I need to audition yardage that would otherwise be too heavy to stay put on its own.

Marking Tools

Every quilter has a favorite marking tool: chalk, air-soluble pens, water-soluble pens, and pencils. A wide variety of tools is available to mark your blocks and quilts, and some tools work better for a particular project than others. Experiment to find out what you like best. Remember to always test your fabric with a marking tool before you begin. From time to time a marking tool will leave a line you drew that is permanent. Taking a few minutes to test how you are going to mark will save you from agonizing over ruined pieces.

Patchwork Seam Guide

A patchwork seam guide is a great tool to have for piecing. The guide on my machine has a small screw to the right of the throat plate that allows the guide to nest next to my 1/4" foot. Other machine models have guides that may attach on the throat or to the presser foot. The guide rail can be pushed against the edge of the presser foot, or at a different distance for larger seam allowances, and fabric cannot extend past the rail. The guide is great when working with small pieces or long seams.

Personal Favorites

In addition to the items previously listed, some of my personal favorite tools that I keep nearby include a seam gauge, an ergonomic seam ripper, a small ruler, and silk pins.

Starch

You will need to use starch or a starch alternative on several of the projects in this book. I like to use Mary Ellen's Best Press. The starch will stiffen the fabric and help control bias pieces, and blocks won't shift as much. Use starch on all the fabrics in your quilt for consistent results. You can wash your quilt after you've finished your project to remove the starch.

Wool Pressing Mat

A wool pressing mat is an optional item, but I'd be remiss not to share that I absolutely love mine! Wool absorbs the moisture in the air, so you don't need to use steam when you press blocks. The wool helps give you a crisp, flat block by working in tandem with your iron to press your blocks from both sides simultaneously. There are pros and cons to using wool mats (they can get stinky) so research before making the investment.

In the know. The Global Organic Textile Standard, or GOTS, is the world's leading processing standard for textiles made with organic fibers. They set standards from harvesting materials through manufacturing, ensuring environmentally and socially responsible practices through the value chain.

As of writing this, the Global Organic Textile Standard organization ended 2022 with 13,549 certified facilities[3]. This is a record high number of certified facilities across the world.

Upcycling

Quilts can be made with anything that a needle can pierce, meaning options for upcycling to make a quilt top are almost limitless. Sheets and clothing are accessible and affordable for most people and can create a variety of texture in a quilt top. You can even upcycle thread!

If you have a quilt that's been well loved, it can easily become a garment or a bag, or be used as batting in a new quilt.

Items that contain synthetics may stretch, so stabilize them with interfacing before cutting pieces and making a quilt or other project.

3. global-standard.org/news/gots-annual-pr-2022

your stash

Organizing Your Fabric

No matter how you choose to organize your stash, the most important thing to keep in mind is that you must be able to see all of your fabric in order to be able to use it for a project. Seeing the fabric in your stash means you make smarter purchasing decisions because you are aware of what you own and are more likely to use it. You spend less time looking for fabric, and it's easier to be intentional about purchases when you know what you already have on your shelves. Ask yourself: *Do I need more or do I want more?* Organizing your stash is key to knowing what you actually need.

There are a lot of ways to organize your stash. I'm sharing what works for me. If you have a system that works, keep using it. If you are still trying to figure out how to store your stash, keep reading! You may need to try organizing a few different ways before you find the method that works best for you and your space. It took time for me to finesse my system, so don't get discouraged if you experiment with several different iterations of fabric organization.

In my studio I organize first by substrate, then by size, and then by hue. I also separate some fabrics by pattern (in my case I have a lot of Asian prints, but maybe you have a lot of batiks or holiday fabrics). I organize precuts and leftover binding separately.

In the know. The textile industry is both water and chemical intensive. Large quantities of fresh water are used for cotton farming, textile printing, dyeing, and finishing, with an estimated 79 billion cubic meters of fresh water used annually across the entire value chain.

Often, water is discharged into rivers and other water sources without treatment. It is estimated that 20 percent of global water pollution is from dyeing and treating textiles.[4]

Sort by Substrate

I separate the substrates, keeping like items together. I primarily have batiks and quilting cotton, but other substrates that I don't use often such as garment and home decor fabrics all have their own section in a cabinet, and I keep interfacing, stabilizer, and muslin in a drawer. Because these other substrates aren't my primary quilting fabrics, I'm comfortable keeping them in a cabinet versus on my shelf because I don't have a lot of them and I can easily inventory the fabrics if I need something in particular.

An assortment of substrates that I store separately from my main stash of quilting cottons.

Sort by Pattern

Sometimes it's a good idea to further subdivide your quilting cottons. For example, I have a large collection of Asian prints and a small amount of solids since I don't use a lot of them. I keep my Asian fabrics on one shelf and solids on another. Perhaps you have a lot of dog and cat fabric, or hearts, or something else you collect. Consider keeping those separate so they are easy to find.

Sort by Fabric Size

Once I have organized my fabric by substrate and pattern, I sort by size using three general size categories: a traditional ¼ yard (9″ × width of fabric) and larger, large scraps and fat quarters, and small scraps and leftover strips of fabric.

I wrap fabric that is a traditional ¼ yard or larger around a comic book board, secured with a rubber band.

4. *European Environmental Agency. The Impact of Textile Production and Waste on the Environment* www.europarl.europa.eu/news/en

Comic book boards are perfect for storing fabric and to use for cardboard templates! They are lightweight, easy to store, and come in packs of 100. Comic book boards are 10½″ high and come in several different widths, making them the perfect size for fabric storage on a bookshelf or on a shelf. I fold yardage into quarters along the width of the fabric (40″/4 = 10″) so it wraps around the board perfectly. Most comic book boards are acid-free, but always make sure so you don't damage your fabric. I wrap a rubber band around my fabric to keep it secure. Rubber bands are easy to get on and off around the comic book board and don't create a sticky mess from tape or result in a finger prick from a straight pin. When the comic book boards wear out, simply recycle or compost them.

I fold fat quarters and larger scraps. There is no rule for what constitutes a large scrap, so use your best judgment.

Small scraps, leftover strips, and small pieces of fabric go into clear bins.

Comic book boards bring uniformity to your fabric storage.

Bindings and Precuts

We all have leftover binding, and it's perfect to keep for small (or large!) projects. I store leftover binding in a clear bin. I don't use a lot of precuts so the small collection I have is in a basket below all my quilting cottons. If you have a large collection of precuts, consider placing them on a shelf or in a cabinet so you can see them.

Sort by Hue

Once I sort by substrate, pattern, and size, I organize by hue. The easiest way to find fabric in your stash is by color. ROYGBIV (red, orange, yellow, green, blue, indigo, and violet) is my guide, but I don't let myself get caught up with fabric being in perfect hue order. I really want pieces to land in the right general area. Fabric sorted by color allows you to easily see what fabrics you may actually need to purchase for a particular project.

How to Use Your Stash Efficiently

Now that you can see your fabric, it's easier to pull for a project. My general rule of thumb is that the more pieces of fabric I have in a quilt, the better. To quote my friend Taffy, "It's not done until it's overdone." When you pull fabric from your stash to make a quilt, pull anything that *might* work. Once you have a stack of possibilities, you can decide to add more from your stash, remove pieces, or recognize there's a fabric you need to purchase to round out the project.

In this photo, I grouped ten fabrics for a quilt. When you use fewer fabrics, color selection matters because your eye has less to look at. Each fabric is important.

In this photo, I curated a selection of 27 fabrics. Because there are so many fabrics, any variations in color matter less because your eye focuses on the overall color theme versus each specific color. *Metaphor* (page 22) is a great example of this. The Log Cabin blocks have color ranges from chartreuse to spring green, aqua green to turquoise, and red-violet to purple to fuchsia to magenta, but together it all works. Your eye sees the color and design, not each individual fabric. In fact, I once had someone ask me what line I used to make *Metaphor* and she was shocked that it wasn't one line but an assortment of scraps.

Supplementing with Intentional Purchases

It is okay to buy new fabric, but be intentional about your purchases. Buy only what you need to finish a project.

Additionally, give yourself permission to replenish what you've used in your stash, but be mindful about what you buy and how much you buy. When considering a purchase, ask yourself a few questions. Do I love this fabric? Is it a color I use frequently? Am I likely to use it? If you answer no to any of these questions, consider not making a purchase. It is possible to go to your local quilt shop and just get inspired.

basic block construction

Seam allowances are ¼″ unless otherwise noted.

Several block components are used throughout this book. For ease, I've shared how to make them here. Refer back to this chapter as needed.

Half-Square Triangles

1. To make a half-square triangle, cut a square in half along the diagonal. **A**

2. Place two triangles, right sides together, and sew together along the long edge. **B**

3. Press and trim to size as needed. **C**

 A
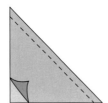 B
 C

Quarter-Square Triangles

1. To make a quarter-square triangle, cut a square in half along both diagonals. **D**

2. Sew 2 sets of 2 triangles, right sides together. Press. **E**

3. Sew the pieced sets, right sides together, to complete the block. Press and trim as needed. **F**

 D
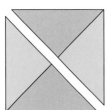 E
 F

Fast Flying Geese

1. Use 1 large square and 4 small squares to make Fast Flying Geese. **A**

2. Place 2 small squares, right sides together, on opposite corners of the larger square. The squares will overlap in the center. Draw a diagonal line from corner to corner through the small squares. Secure the squares with pins. Sew ¼″ from each side of the diagonal line. **B**

3. Cut along the diagonal line. Press the smaller triangles away from the larger triangle, forming 2 heart-shaped pieces. **C–D**

4. Place a small square on the corner of each larger triangle, right sides together. Draw a diagonal line across the square. Secure with a pin. Sew ¼″ from each side of the diagonal line. **E**

5. Cut along the diagonal line. Press toward the small triangle. Trim to size as needed. **F**

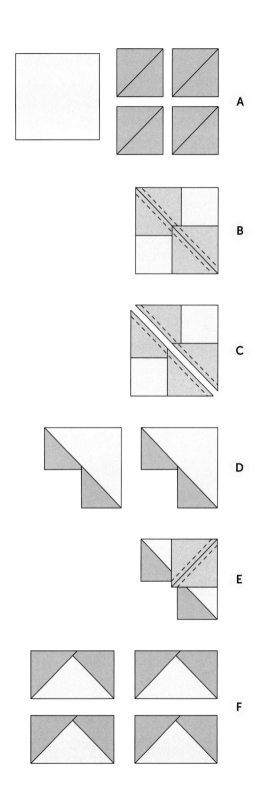

Square-in-a-Square

1. Cut 2 squares in half along the diagonal.

2. Sew a half-square triangle (page 16) to opposite sides of a larger square. Press. **A–B**

3. Sew a half-square triangle to the remaining sides of the block. Press and trim to size as needed. **C**

To make a square-in-a-square-in-a-square, add another set of half-square triangles around all 4 sides of the square-in-a-square block. Press and trim. **D–E**

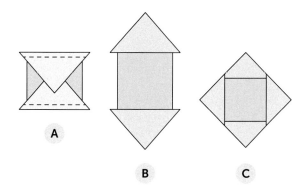

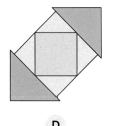

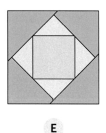

How to Miter Corners

When you miter a border, you create a 45° seam in each corner. When you do this, you need your border strips to be longer than the finished length of a straight border. The formula is length plus double the border width (including the seam allowances) plus another few inches. Generally, if I miter a narrow border, I add an inch or two, and if I miter a wider border, I add two to three inches extra, and more if the border is really wide!

For example, if you want a 4″ finished, mitered border on a 60″ × 75″ quilt, you will need to cut two sets of border strips.

60½″ + 4½″ + 4½″ + 2″ extra = 71½″, so round up to cut 2 strips 4½″ × 72″

and

75½″ + 4½″ + 4½″ + 2″ extra = 86½″, so round up to cut 2 strips 4½″ × 87″

1. Cut strips to the desired length.

2. Mark both the quilt and the border strips at the center. Pin the border to opposite sides of the quilt at the center and along the edge.

3. Start and stop sewing ¼″ from each corner. I recommend you lock the seam by backstitching a few stitches. Press. **A–B**

4. Repeat on the 2 remaining sides. **C–D**

5. Fold the corner of the quilt onto itself at a 45° angle, aligning the border edges. **E**

6. Align a ruler with the folded edge of the quilt. **F**

7. Draw a line from the end of the stitches on your border to the outer edge. Pin the borders together. **G**

8. Sew along the line, backstitching where the borders meet at the inside of the quilt and the outer edge. Trim to a ¼″ seam allowance and press. **H–I**

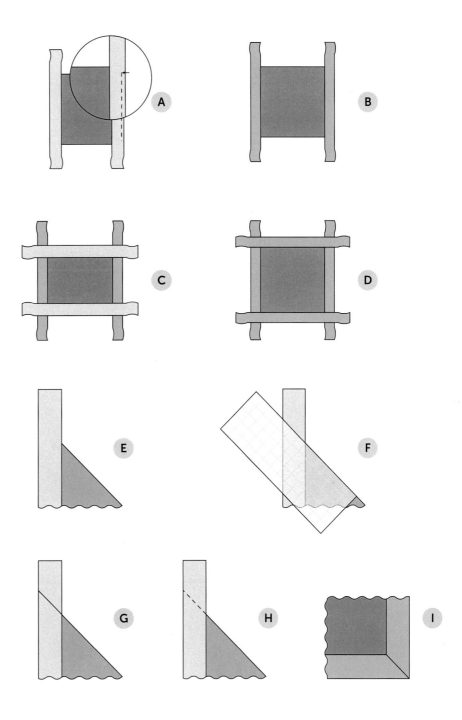

⟨⟨ The Earth is what we all have in common." **WENDELL BERRY**

before you begin

The idea behind this book is twofold—use the fabric you have in your stash before purchasing new fabric to make quilts *and/or* if you buy fabric, use it in its entirety. There are four main quilt projects in this book. Each of these projects also features a number of subsequent projects that can be made with the pieces of leftover fabric from the main quilt. If you choose to make the main quilt and then each of the subprojects in turn, you will end up with minimal or no scraps.

Each subproject lists yardage requirements, so you can choose to make it separately. However, you may end up with scraps remaining because you aren't starting with the original project.

The projects in this book are based on 40″-wide fabric, and I added enough to cut at least 1 more of the widest strip to my fabric requirements to allow for fabric shrinkage and occasional miscuts. Many secondary projects require the addition of a little more yardage in order to use all the original materials. The extra fabric requirements are minimal, and you will likely be able to round out additional project needs from your stash.

Because of miscuts, fabric shrinking, and other hiccups that happen when we sew, I introduce what I call "creative cutting" in this book. You will have enough fabric to make the primary projects, but the secondary projects may require you to think differently about how you cut materials.

The leftover projects are guidelines for you to use the remaining fabric, and there are some assumptions I make about creating supplemental projects. If you didn't miscut, make a change in the design, or experience any other hiccup, and if your fabric isn't wildly off grain, you should have enough fabric to make all the remaining projects. However, if the fabric I used has a smaller or larger selvage than a fabric you use for your project, you may end up with slightly more or less fabric to make supplemental items. Keep in mind that it's easy to add a fabric or adjust your design slightly to make additional things *and* that each project has its own materials requirement so you can make items as an intentional set or individually.

If you find you have more, or less, of a fabric, or fabrics, adjust the design. Make 6″ coasters instead of 5″ coasters; add another row of half-square triangles to your zipper pouches. The idea is that, while there are patterns to follow, they can also be used as a guideline for you. Allow yourself to get creative with what you make. If nothing else, it's a great exercise in the creative process.

All projects assume waste at scraps measuring less than 1″ × 1″.

I prefer to make bias-cut quilt binding, unless otherwise noted in the projects. The yardage noted for the binding is enough to cut 2″-wide binding on the bias or on the straight grain.

Enter the Scrap Bag

I keep a fabric scrap bag next to my cutting table to fill with small bits of fabric and thread left when I trim or square up yardage and blocks. The pieces are tiny, usually less than ⅛″ wide, but over time it accumulates. When I have enough, I make a muslin pillow form (usually a 12″ square or other standard size) and stuff it with the scraps. The pillow form can sit on a shelf until I'm ready to use it. Likewise, you can just keep a bag of scraps and use them for any other project, like stuffing a toy animal or pincushion. You can also compost the scraps! Cotton fabric (or any other natural fiber) will disintegrate over time in your garden. Be aware that some dyes can be toxic so cut around any heavily printed areas, like a t-shirt logo or graphic, and don't put those in the compost pile. Additionally, if the fabric is heavily printed you should find another way to repurpose or recycle it.

In the know. Pollution isn't new. Fermenting woad, a plant that yields a blue dye, was so smelly that Queen Elizabeth I issued a proclamation banning it from being fermented within an 8-mile radius of any of her palaces.[5]

---

5. Virginia Postrel. *The Fabric of Civilization* 2020, page 115.

Metaphor

FINISHED BLOCK: 3¾˝ × 3¾˝ • FINISHED QUILT: 56¾˝ × 60½˝

METAPHOR BEGAN AS AN EXERCISE IN SCRAP MANAGEMENT. SEVERAL YEARS ago, I cut and gathered a myriad of fabric scraps and put them into four color groups. After looking at bags of strips for a few weeks, I decided they would make a colorful Log Cabin.

This quilt sat half-finished for a few years. When I picked it back up to finish the top, I absent-mindedly pieced my logs going different directions, so instead of the pieces all going left to right, or vice versa, they went left to right *and* right to left. Instead of starting over or separating the blocks into like directions, I decided to go with it. There was absolute freedom piecing this way! Blocks came together in a unique pattern on my design wall, and, when this was pieced in late 2022, the quilt became a metaphor for what was going on in the world. I knew how blocks in a traditional Log Cabin should come together to create a pattern, and everything was pieced correctly, but they weren't quite right—some were backward. Familiar, but not normal.

I had to purchase backing fabric to finish this quilt.

Materials

Yardages are based on 40˝-wide fabrics.

Center/Gray: ⅓ yard

Purple: ⅞ yard

Blue: 1⅔ yards

Pink: 1¾ yards

Green: 2⅛ yards

Backing: 3¾ yards

Binding: ⅝ yard
for bias binding

Batting: 65˝ × 69˝

Cutting

There are eleven block combinations, and most have a clockwise and a counterclockwise construction. Be sure to keep small and large cuts separate. Block construction quantities are noted in the assembly instructions.

Center

Cut 240 squares
1¼˝ × 1¼˝.

Purple

Cut 16 strips 1¼˝ × WOF.
Subcut into:

27 squares 1¼˝ × 1¼˝

53 rectangles 1¼˝ × 2˝

53 rectangles 1¼˝ × 2¾˝

53 rectangles 1¼˝ × 3½˝

26 rectangles 1¼˝ × 4¼˝

Blue

Cut 41 strips 1¼˝ × WOF.
Subcut into:

75 squares 1¼˝ × 1¼˝

139 rectangles 1¼˝ × 2˝

139 rectangles
1¼˝ × 2¾˝

139 rectangles
1¼˝ × 3½˝

64 rectangles 1¼˝ × 4¼˝

Pink

Cut 39 strips 1¼˝ × WOF.
Subcut into:

61 squares 1¼˝ × 1¼˝

129 rectangles 1¼˝ × 2˝

129 rectangles
1¼˝ × 2¾˝

129 rectangles 1¼˝ × 3½˝

68 rectangles 1¼˝ × 4¼˝

Green

Cut 48 strips 1¼˝ × WOF.
Subcut into:

77 squares 1¼˝ × 1¼˝

159 rectangles 1¼˝ × 2˝

159 rectangles
1¼˝ × 2¾˝

159 rectangles
1¼˝ × 3½˝

82 rectangles 1¼˝ × 4¼˝

Construction

Seam allowances are ¼″ unless otherwise noted.

Block Assembly

You will make 240 Log Cabin blocks with an unfinished size of 4¼″ × 4¼″. Please follow the block layout diagrams.

1. Blocks are sewn together in a clockwise or counterclockwise manner.

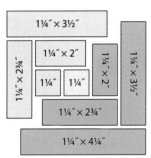

Clockwise

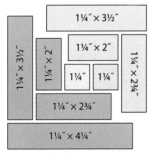

Counterclockwise

2. Sew blocks together as shown in the diagrams. Press seams away from the center square.

3. Make blocks in the following color combinations:

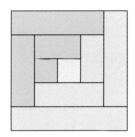

Make 12

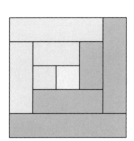

Make 7

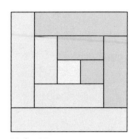

Make 27

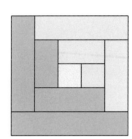

Make 31

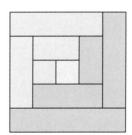

Make 4

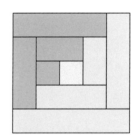

Make 5

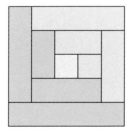

Make 16

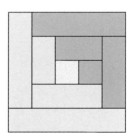

Make 25

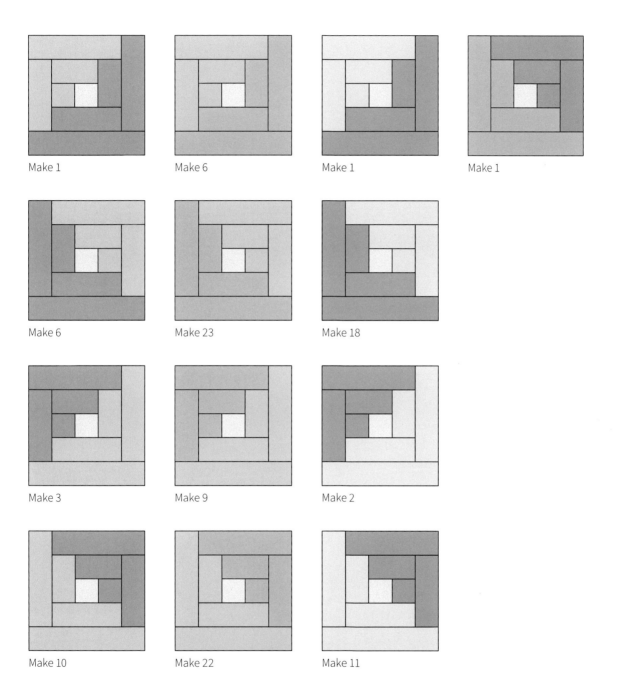

Make 1

Make 6

Make 1

Make 1

Make 6

Make 23

Make 18

Make 3

Make 9

Make 2

Make 10

Make 22

Make 11

Quilt Construction

1. Arrange the blocks according to the quilt diagram.

2. Sew the blocks into rows. Press.

3. Sew the rows together. Press.

Finishing

Quilt, bind, and enjoy!

In the know. It takes between two and three years to transition cotton from traditionally grown to organic. The cotton produced during this time is known as "in-conversion" or "transitional."

QUILT ASSEMBLY

Sawing Logs

FINISHED BLOCKS: 12½″ × 12½″ • FINISHED QUILT: 64¼″ × 79½″

Quilted by Cheryl Ashley-Serafine

I REALLY LIKE THIS QUILT BECAUSE IT SHOWS YOU HOW TO TAKE SMALL BLOCKS and put them into a cohesive, well-thought-out larger quilt. Adding fabric that coordinates with the Log Cabins gives the quilt more dimension, and since the quilt is scrappy, it all comes together because the colors play nicely together. I added some more purple, blue, and pink fabrics to make the blocks more fun, which gave me more fabric for the next projects.

Materials

Yardages are based on 40˝-wide fabrics.

If Starting with Leftovers

Gather leftovers and other scraps or pieces to be cut into the shapes noted in the Cutting list.

Purple: 1 strip 50½˝ × WOF or equivalent

Blue: 1 strip 58¼˝ × WOF or equivalent

Pink: 1 strip 57˝ × WOF or equivalent

Green: 1 strip 3¾˝ × WOF or equivalent

If Starting with Yardage

Purple: 1½ yards

Blue: 1¾ yards

Pink: 1¾ yards

Green: ¼ yard

Additional Materials
FOR BOTH LEFTOVERS AND YARDAGE

Background: 3½ yards

Binding: ⅝ yard

Backing: 5 yards

Batting: 73˝ × 88˝

Cutting

Purple

From leftovers or new yardage cut the following for Log Cabin blocks:

Cut 3 strips 1¼˝ × WOF. Subcut into:

>   5 strips 1¼˝ × 4¼˝
>   9 strips 1¼˝ × 3½˝
>   9 strips 1¼˝ × 2¾˝
>   9 rectangles 1¼˝ × 2˝
>   4 squares 1¼˝ × 1¼˝

Cut the following for the Flying Geese and block borders:

Cut 3 strips 3½˝ × WOF. Subcut into 24 squares 3½˝ × 3½˝.

From the remaining 3½˝ × 33˝ strip. Subcut:

>   2 rectangles 1¾˝ × 33, then subcut:
>   2 rectangles 1¾˝ × 13˝ and 2 rectangles 1¾˝ × 10½˝

Cut 7 strips 1¾˝ × WOF. Subcut into:

>   10 rectangles 1¾˝ × 13˝
>   10 rectangles 1¾˝ × 10½˝

Blue

From leftovers or new yardage cut the following for Log Cabin blocks:

Cut 4 strips 1¼˝ × WOF. Subcut into:

>   8 rectangles 1¼˝ × 4¼˝
>   13 rectangles 1¼˝ × 3½˝
>   13 rectangles 1¼˝ × 2¾˝
>   13 rectangles 1¼˝ × 2˝
>   5 squares 1¼˝ × 1¼˝

Cut the following for the Flying Geese and block borders:

Cut 3 strips 3½˝ × WOF. Subcut into 28 squares 3½˝ × 3½˝.

From the remaining 3½˝ × 19˝ strips, subcut 2 rectangles 1¾˝ × 13˝.

Cut 9 strips 1¾˝ × WOF. Subcut into:

>   12 rectangles 1¾˝ × 13˝
>   14 rectangles 1¾˝ × 10½˝

Pink

From leftovers or new yardage cut the following for Log Cabin blocks:

Cut 3 strips 1¼˝ × WOF. Subcut into:

>   5 rectangles 1¼˝ × 4¼˝
>   10 rectangles 1¼˝ × 3½˝
>   10 rectangles 1¼˝ × 2¾˝
>   10 rectangles 1¼˝ × 2˝
>   5 squares 1¼˝ × 1¼˝

Cut the following for the Flying Geese and block borders:

Cut 3 strips 3½˝ × WOF. Subcut into 28 squares 3½˝ × 3½˝.

From the remaining 3½˝ × 19˝ strips, subcut 2 rectangles 1¾˝ × 13˝.

Cut 9 strips 1¾˝ × WOF. Subcut into:

>   14 rectangles 1¾˝ × 10½˝
>   12 rectangles 1¾˝ × 13˝

Green

From leftovers or new yardage cut the following for Log Cabin blocks:

Cut 3 strips 1¼˝ × WOF. Subcut into:

>   6 squares 1¼˝ × 1¼˝
>   8 rectangles 1¼˝ × 2˝
>   8 rectangles 1¼˝ × 2¾˝
>   8 rectangles 1¼˝ × 3½˝
>   2 rectangles 1¼˝ × 4¼˝

Background

Cut 4 strips 6½˝ × WOF. Subcut into 20 squares 6½˝ × 6½˝.

From remaining 6½˝ × 27˝ strip, subcut 4 rectangles 3¼˝ × 13˝.

Cut 13 strips 3¼˝ × WOF. Trim off selvages and sew together then cut:

>   2 rectangles 3¼˝ × 79½˝
>   6 rectangles 3¼˝ × 58¾˝

Cut 4 strips 3¼˝ × WOF. Subcut into 11 rectangles 3¼˝ × 13˝.

Cut 4 strips 3¼˝ × WOF. Subcut into 40 squares 3¼˝ × 3¼˝, then cut into half-square triangles.

Cut 7 strips 3˝ × WOF. Subcut 80 squares 3˝ × 3˝.

Construction

Seam allowances are ¼˝ unless otherwise noted.

Block Assembly

MAKE THE LOG CABINS

1. Make 20 Log Cabin blocks with finished size 3¾˝ × 3¾˝ using the 1¼˝ strips. Follow the *Metaphor* Block Assembly instructions (page 24) to make your blocks.

Make the following combinations; they can be clockwise or counterclockwise, your choice!

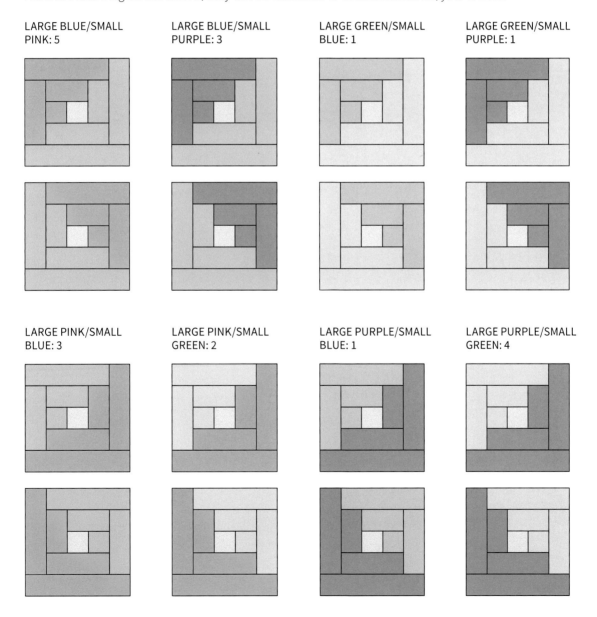

LARGE BLUE/SMALL PINK: 5

LARGE BLUE/SMALL PURPLE: 3

LARGE GREEN/SMALL BLUE: 1

LARGE GREEN/SMALL PURPLE: 1

LARGE PINK/SMALL BLUE: 3

LARGE PINK/SMALL GREEN: 2

LARGE PURPLE/SMALL BLUE: 1

LARGE PURPLE/SMALL GREEN: 4

2. Sew a 3¼″ half-square triangle onto 2 opposite sides of the Log Cabin blocks. Press. **A**

3. Repeat Step 2 for remaining 2 sides of each block. Press. Center block will measure 5½″ × 5½″. **B**

MAKE FLYING GEESE

1. Follow Fast Flying Geese instructions on page 17 to make 20 sets of 4 Fast Flying Geese. Use 1 square 6½″ × 6½″ and 4 squares 3½″ × 3½″ to make the blocks.

2. Trim the Flying Geese to 3″ × 5½″, keeping the ¼″ seam at the top of the triangle.

3. Match the sets of Flying Geese and frames to the block centers.

ASSEMBLE THE BLOCKS

1. Sew a Flying Geese unit to 2 sides of each center block. Press. **C**

2. Sew 2 squares 3″ × 3″ to the ends of 2 Flying Geese of each set. Press. **D**

3. Sew the unit from Step 2 onto the remaining sides of the unit from Step 1 to complete the block. **E**

4. Sew a 1¾″ × 10½″ frame to each side of the block. Press.

5. Sew a 1¾″ × 13″ frame to the remaining two sides of the block. Press.

Quilt Construction

1. Arrange the blocks into 5 rows of 4 blocks each.

2. Sew a 3¼″ × 13″ sashing strip between the blocks in each row. Press. **F**

3. Sew a 3¼″ × 58¾″ sashing strip between each row and a border to the top and bottom rows. Press.

4. Sew the rows together.

5. Sew a 3¼″ × 79½″ border to the outside edges. Press.

6. Quilt, bind, and enjoy!

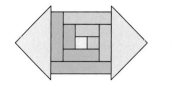

A

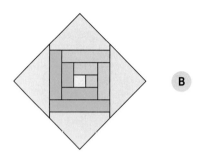

B

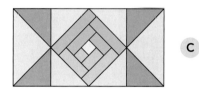

C

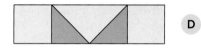

D

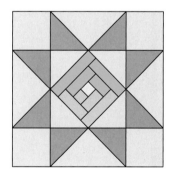

E

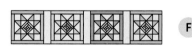

F

QUILT ASSEMBLY

Best Foot Forward

FINISHED BAG: 15¼" × 16⅜"

ANOTHER FAVORITE PROJECT—THIS DARLING SHOE BAG! I'M A BIG FAN OF SHOE
bags when I travel because they keep my clothing clean.

I had a few larger scraps and decided to make this so I didn't have to cut the fabric down further.
This shoe bag comes together in a half hour, so it's fast to make. I used a piece of ribbon in my
ribbon collection to round out the project.

Materials

Yardages are based on 40″-wide fabrics.

If Starting with Leftovers

Leftover 4½″ × WOF strip from *Sawing Logs*

Leftover 5″ × WOF strip from *Sawing Logs*

Leftover 7″ × WOF strip from *Metaphor*

2 leftover sashing rectangles 3¼″ × 16″ from *Sawing Logs*

If Starting with Yardage

Fabric 1: ¼ yard

Fabric 2: ¼ yard

Fabric 3: ⅜ yard

Additional Materials
FOR BOTH LEFTOVERS AND YARDAGE

2 yards ribbon or other trim for bag closure

Cutting

If Starting with Leftovers

Cut a 31″ strip from each leftover piece of fabric for the bag.

If Starting with Yardage

FABRIC 1

Cut a 4½″ × 31″ rectangle of fabric for the bag.

FABRIC 2

Cut a 5″ × 31″ rectangle for the bag.

FABRIC 3

Cut a 7″ × 31″ rectangle for the bag.

Cut 2 rectangles 3¼″ × 16″ for the casing.

Ribbon

Cut ribbon or other trim into 2 pieces 1 yard each.

Construction

Seam allowances are ¼″ unless otherwise noted.

Making the Bag Body

Sew the long edges of the rectangles together to make a 15½″ × 31″ panel.

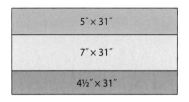

If you have a serger, you can serge the edges to finish or you can finish the seams by sewing together with a ⅜″ seam, then with a zigzag stitch. You can also sew the seams together with a French seam to prevent fraying.

Make the Casing

1. Serge or zigzag the 3¼″ edges of the casing strips. Hem these edges by folding them ½″ to the wrong side and edgestitch a ¼″ from each edge to secure. **A**

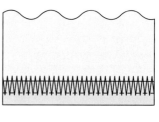

2. Press the casing strip in half lengthwise, wrong sides together.

3. Zigzag the long edge of the strip to prevent fraying if you are not using a serger. If you are using a serger to sew the bag together, move to the next step.

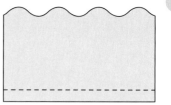

A

Make the Shoe Bag

1. Mark the center of the bag with a straight pin or chalk, or by pressing a crease. **B**

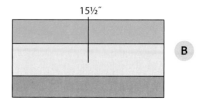

B

2. Center each casing along the top of each half of the bag. There will be a ½″ gap in the center of the bag and the casings will be ¼″ short of the outer edges. **C**

3. Sew the casing to the bag using a ¼″ seam, or serge together. Press seam toward the bottom of the bag and edgestitch ⅛″ from the seam, stitching the seam allowance down.

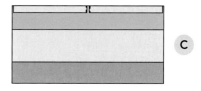

C

4. Fold the shoe bag in half, right sides together. Sew the bottom and unfinished side of the shoe bag together. You can serge or zigzag the edges to finish.

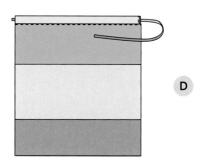

D

5. Place a safety pin in one end of a piece of ribbon. Thread a ribbon through both casings, then tie together with a simple overhand knot. **D–E**

6. Repeat Step 5 with the second ribbon in the opposite direction so you have a knot on each side of the bag.

7. Fill bag with shoes and enjoy!

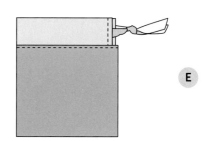

E

Cute as Pie Carrier

FINISHED BLOCK: 4½" × 4½" • FINISHED CARRIER: 18½" × 18½"

ORIGINALLY, I WAS PLAYING AROUND WITH THE LEFTOVERS AND MADE SOME wonky Log Cabins using leftover scraps of fabric. However, when the blocks were finished, I wasn't happy (I'd managed to make a creepy doll quilt!), so I cut them into quarter-square triangles, rearranged them, and sewed the pieces back together. The end result is a fun and bright pie, or small casserole, carrier.

I had to buy the cotton webbing but the interfacing, insulated batting, and backing were all in my stash.

Materials

Yardages are based on 40″-wide fabrics.

If Starting with Leftovers

Assorted strips in a variety of lengths and widths from *Metaphor* and *Sawing Logs*

1¾″ strips from block borders from *Sawing Logs*

3¼″ sashing strips from *Sawing Logs*

If Starting with Yardage

Fabric 1: ¼ yard

Fabric 2: ¼ yard

Fabric 3: ¼ yard

Fabric 4: ⅓ yard

Additional Materials
FOR BOTH LEFTOVERS AND YARDAGE

Lining: ⅝ yard

Woven fusible interfacing: ⅝ yard

Batting or insulated batting: ⅝ yard

1½″ cotton webbing for handles: 1¼ yards

Starch or starch alternative

TIP
You may also use an 18½″ × 18½″ square of fabric or any block this size for the top of the pie carrier if you don't want to make the improv Log Cabin blocks. If you choose to do this, proceed to Make the Carrier (page 38).

Cutting

If Starting with Leftovers

Cut 10 squares 3¼″ × 3¼″ from the *Sawing Logs* leftover sashing strips.

If Starting with Yardage

FABRIC 1

Cut 2 strips 1¼″ × WOF.

Cut 1 strip 1½″ × WOF.

Cut 1 strip 1¾″ × WOF.

FABRIC 2

Cut 1 strip 1½″ × WOF.

Cut 2 strips 1¾″ × WOF.

FABRIC 3

Cut 2 strips 1¼″ × WOF.

Cut 1 strip 1½″ × WOF.

Cut 2 strips 1¾″ × WOF.

FABRIC 4

Cut 1 strip 3¼″ × WOF. Subcut 10 squares 3¼″ × 3¼″.

Cut 3 strips 1¼″ × WOF.

Cut 1 strip 1½″ × WOF.

Cut 1 strip 1¾″ × WOF.

Lining and Batting

Cut 1 square 18½″ × 18½″ from each.

Interfacing

Cut 2 squares 18½″ × 18½″.

Cotton Webbing

Cut 2 strips 10″ long and 1 strip 22″ long.

Construction

Seam allowances are ¼″ unless otherwise noted.

Make the Log Cabin or Court House Step Blocks

The improv Log Cabin or Court House Step blocks are made by sewing different-width strips around or on opposite sides of the 3¾″ × 3¾″ center. If you are using leftover strips, use the shortest-length pieces first and build the block out with larger pieces on the outside edges.

Build each block to a square 8″ × 8″. You will make 10 blocks. Two of the blocks will be used for the *Coffee Goes Here* mug rugs (page 39).

If you are using WOF strips, randomly use the different widths of fabric to build out the block. Keep any leftovers you trim that have one side that measures 1½″ wide for the *Coffee Goes Here* mug rugs (page 39).

Each block will be different and may vary slightly from mine, depending on what pieces you have remaining after you make *Metaphor* and *Sawing Logs*.

Remember, if you miscut and are a little bit short, just throw in another piece of fabric to round out the project.

Here are three examples of how blocks *might* look when they are pieced.

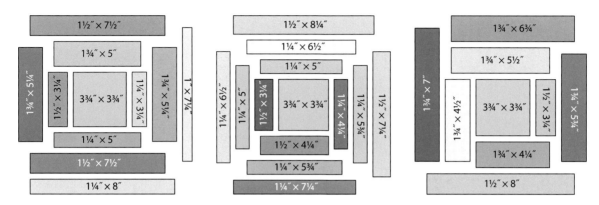

Starch each block before you trim and shuffle them in the next steps.

TRIM AND SHUFFLE BLOCKS

Refer to Basic Block Construction (page 16) for half-square triangle and quarter-square triangle instructions.

1. Cut each improv Log Cabin block into quarter-square triangles. **A**

2. Make a half-square triangle block by sewing two different quarter-square triangle units together along the long edge. Press and trim each block to 5″ × 5″. **B–C**

3. Arrange 16 blocks in a 4 × 4 grid to your liking and sew them together to make the top of the pie carrier. **D**

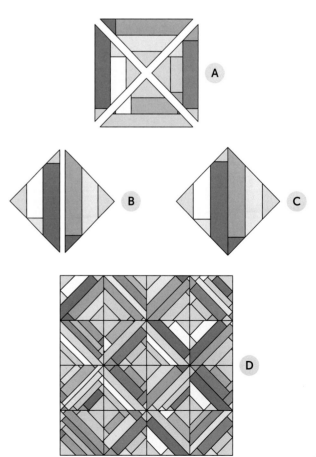

Make the Carrier

1. Iron the fusible interfacing to the *wrong* side of the pie carrier top block (or square) and the lining square.

2. Measure 3″ from each corner. Draw a diagonal line between the marks, then cut along the line to remove the corner. Fold the cut edge in half and crease to mark the center.

3. Repeat Step 2 for the lining fabric and the insulated batting. **A–B**

4. Turn the trimmed carrier top face up and center the 22″ cotton webbing diagonally across the carrier. Pin or thread baste the edges. **C**

5. Fold a piece of 10″ cotton webbing and place the ends on either side of the center crease on a remaining corner and pin or thread baste into place. Repeat for the second handle. **D**

6. Place the lining fabric on top of the carrier top, right sides together. Place the batting on top of the lining fabric. If using insulated batting, the silver foil side should be next to the back side of the lining fabric. **E**

7. Secure the edges with clips or pins. Sew around the edges of the carrier, leaving a 4″ opening to turn the carrier right side out. **F**

8. Clip the corners, then turn the carrier right side out and press. Whipstitch the opening closed. **F**

9. Enjoy!

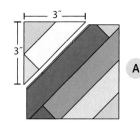

A

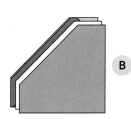

B

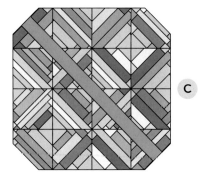

C

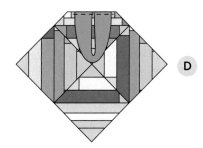

D

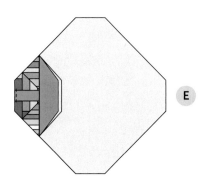

E

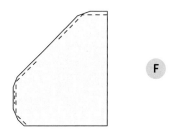

F

Coffee Goes Here

FINISHED MAT: 7″ × 7″

WHAT TO DO WITH FOUR EXTRA HALF-SQUARE TRIANGLE BLOCKS? I MEAN, REALLY.
It stumped me until I realized I could sew the pieces together to make some adorable mug rugs. And two mug rugs are better than one because then you can have coffee with a friend. Or give as a gift. Or both!

I backed the mug rugs with scrap fabric and used leftover binding from *Metaphor*.

Materials

Yardages are based on 40˝-wide fabrics.

If Starting with Leftovers

4 half-square triangle blocks from *Cute as Pie Carrier*

An assortment of scraps that measure 1½˝ on any one side

If Starting with Yardage

Yardages are based on 40˝ wide materials.

⅔ yard assorted scraps

Additional Materials
FOR BOTH LEFTOVERS AND YARDAGE

Binding: 2 strips 2˝ × WOF *or* scrap bias binding

Batting: 2 squares 7˝ × 7˝

Cutting

Cut 4 center squares 3¼˝ × 3¼˝.
Cut 8 rectangles 1⅞˝ × 8˝.
Cut 8 rectangles 1⅞˝ × 5¾˝.
Cut 8 rectangles 1¾˝ × 5¾˝.
Cut 8 rectangles 1¾˝ × 3¼˝.
Cut an assortment of scraps any width by 1½˝ high.

Construction

Seam allowances are ¼˝ unless otherwise noted.

Make the Blocks

If you are using leftover half-square triangles, proceed to Make the Half-Square Triangle Blocks.

1. Sew the blocks together as follows to make 4 blocks 8˝ × 8˝. **A**

2. Cut each block into quarter-square triangles. **B**

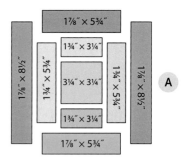

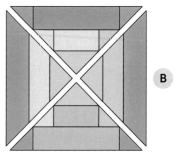

MAKE THE HALF-SQUARE TRIANGLE BLOCKS

Sew 2 half-square triangle sections together to create a half-square triangle block. Make 4 half-square triangle blocks. Trim to 5″ × 5″. **C–D**

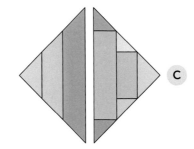 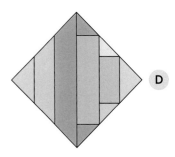

Make the Pieced Border

1. Sew the 1½″-tall leftover scraps together to make the border. The pieces will vary in width but should all measure 1½″ in height. You should have enough to make 4 strips 1½″ × approximately 24″. **E**

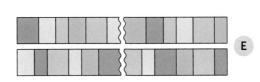

2. From each border strip, cut 2 border rectangles 1½″ × 5″ and 2 border rectangles 1½″ × 7″.

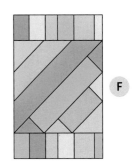

Attach the Border Strips

1. Sew the 1½″ × 5″ border strips to opposite sides of the blocks. **F**

2. Sew the 1½″ × 7″ border strips to remaining two sides of the blocks. **G**

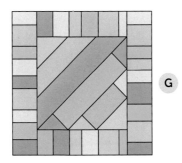

Finishing

1. Quilt and bind as desired.

2. Enjoy!

Wipe Your Face

FINISHED WIPES: 2½˝ × 2½˝

ORIGINALLY, WHEN I PLANNED TO MAKE THE PIE CARRIER, I WASN'T GOING TO trim off the corners. After my design changed, I was left with small half-square triangles. Fortunately, the triangles from the cover and the lining fabric were the same size, but what to make with 4 squares 2½˝ each? Reusable makeup wipes, perfect for removing eye makeup, of course! I'm grateful that the idea came to me quickly, and these are so fast and easy to make!

These cleaning wipes were completed using scraps of flannel from my stash, and, while these are small, you can use the same technique for any size of cloth. Scraps of flannel, microfiber, and old towels are perfect for one or both sides. You can serge, pink, or use a binding along the edges, or you can sew the pieces right sides together, turn, and edgestitch for a more finished look.

Materials

Yardages are based on 40″-wide fabrics.

If Starting with Leftovers

8 half-square triangle leftovers from the *Cute As Pie Carrier*

If Starting with Yardage

⅛ yard assorted scraps

Additional Materials
FOR BOTH LEFTOVERS AND YARDAGE

Backing: ⅛ yard flannel, terry cloth, or microfiber

Cutting

Cut 4 squares 3″ × 3″ from assorted scraps. Subcut into half-square triangles.

Cut 4 squares 2½″ × 2½″ from flannel, terry cloth, or other backing fabric.

Construction

Seam allowances are ¼″ unless otherwise noted.

Refer to Basic Block Construction (page 16) for half-square instructions.

Make the Squares

1. Sew 2 half-square triangle units together. Press. Trim to 2½″ × 2½″. **A**

2. Repeat Step 1 to make 4 blocks.

MAKE THE COTTON WIPES

1. Place a half-square triangle block, *wrong sides together*, with your backing piece (flannel, terry cloth, microfiber).

2. Sew a ¼″ seam around the cloth. Pink the edges to prevent fraying. **B**

3. Enjoy!

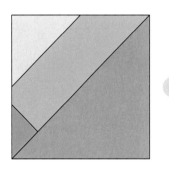

A

B

Weighed Down

FINISHED SIZE: 2¾" × 2¾"

GOOD THINGS COME IN SETS OF THREE, AND PATTERN WEIGHTS ARE NO
exception. I always need more, especially if I'm cutting out a skirt—ask me how I know. One
leftover strip of fabric was exactly what I needed to make these little weights. I filled mine with
sawdust, but you can use anything you'd like.

Materials

If Starting with Leftovers

Yardages are based on 40˝-wide fabrics.

1 rectangle 3¼˝ × 19½˝ from *Metaphor*

If Starting with Yardage

⅛ yard fabric

Additional Materials

FOR BOTH LEFTOVERS AND YARDAGE

⅜˝ ribbon: ⅓ yard, or equivalent fabric scrap

Sawdust or other filling of choice

Cutting

Cut 6 squares 3¼˝ × 3¼˝.
Cut 3 strips of ribbon 4˝ long.

66 The greatest threat to our planet is the belief that someone else will save it." ROBERT SWAN

Construction

Seam allowances are ¼˝ unless otherwise noted.

1. If you've opted to use a fabric scrap instead of a ribbon, fold it lengthwise, right sides together, and sew along the long side. Turn right side out and press.

2. Fold the ribbon or fabric strip from Step 1 in half and place ⅜˝ from one corner of the right side of a 3¼˝ × 3¼˝ square, and pin. **A**

3. Place another 3¼˝ × 3¼˝ square, right sides together, on top of the first square. Sew around 3 sides of the square. **B**

4. On the open side, match the two center seams to create a triangle. Sew from one edge to the center. Backstitch when you start and stop to secure the seam. **C**

5. Turn the pattern weight right side out and fill with sawdust or other filling of choice.

6. Close the opening to secure.

7. Enjoy!

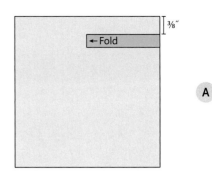

A

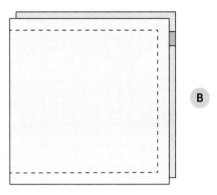

B

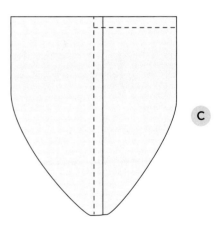

C

They Got Married

FINISHED BLOCK: 22″ x 22″ • FINISHED QUILT: 88½″ x 88½″

Quilted by Cheryl Ashley-Serafine

I FELL IN LOVE WITH JENNIFER SAMPOU'S SKY OMBRÉ FABRICS AFTER MAKING
another quilt using that line. Creating *They Got Married* was an exercise in patience and color, but the results are worth it! This double wedding ring is created with floral arcs, ombré melons, and ombré center pieces. The color moves and flows like a rainbow. I used large- and small-scale florals, geometric prints, and polka dots to create the effect.

This quilt uses a substantial amount of fabric and leaves some oddly shaped scraps, but I created eight additional innovative projects that use up the remaining fabric. I found ingenious ways to work with angled scraps to maximize fabric use.

The majority of the florals were from scraps in my stash, and I used some scrap bias binding. I had to purchase a few small quantities of fabric to complete my binding, and I purchased the ombré and backing fabric.

Materials

Yardages are based on 40˝-wide fabrics.

11 yards assorted florals for the ring arcs and joining squares*

28 assorted half-yard ombré cuts in a variety of colors for block centers and melons

Backing: 8¼ yards

Binding: ¾ yard for bias binding

Batting: 97˝ × 97˝

*If you opt to use scraps or fat quarters, like I did, what you really need will be 128 rectangles 6˝ × 16˝.

Cutting

Important: Cut the arcs and arrange them on a design wall *before* you cut your melons and center pieces, making sure the color flows from arc to arc first. Color placement is crucial for this quilt and even small changes in arc placement can affect what color melon and center you use. After you have your arcs arranged, cut the larger center pieces, then the smaller melons.

TIP

Lightly starch the fabric before cutting the strips to minimize stretch.

Assorted Florals

Cut 16˝ × WOF strips. Subcut 6 rectangles 6˝ × 16˝. From each rectangle cut 1 arc using the Arc A template (page 124) and 2 squares 2⅜˝ × 2⅜˝.

There is little room for error so cut carefully. This layout preserves the largest areas for triangles needed in later projects.

Ombrés

Cut 64 melons using Melon B template (page 124).

Cut 25 large center background pieces using Center C template (page 125).

Cut 12 side setting pieces using Side D template (page 124).

Construction

Seam allowances are ¼″ unless otherwise noted.

Make the Melons

1. Fold and finger-press to find the center of an arc and the center of a melon. Pin together at the center and at each end. **A**

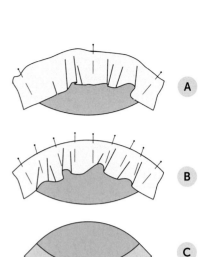

2. Keeping the seam allowances aligned, pin the arc to the melon, distributing the fullness of the melon evenly. **B**

3. Sew the arc and melon together. I like to sew these pieces together with the arc on top. Use a stiletto to keep the pieces lined up, if needed. Go slow and make sure you take the pins out of the fabric before they go under the presser foot. Press. **C**

4. Sew a 2⅜″ × 2⅜″ square to each end of the arc for the opposite side of the melon. Press. **D**

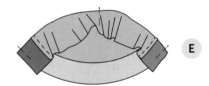

5. Finger-press to find the center of the second arc and the other side of the melon. Pin together at the center and at each end. Ease the remaining arc fullness to match the melon and pin as needed. Sew together to make a complete melon. Press. **E–F**

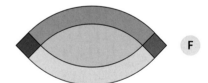

TIP
You may need to clip the curves of melon pieces if they appear stretched.

6. Repeat Steps 1–5 to sew the remaining melons.

Make the Blocks

1. Finger-press to find the center of a completed melon and the center of one side of a background piece. Pin together at the center and at the ends, allowing the ¼″ seam allowance of the background piece to extend past the seam line of the square. Sew the pieces together and press. **G**

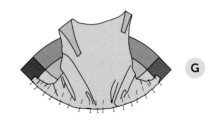

2. Repeat Step 1 for the remaining three sides to make a complete circle. **H**

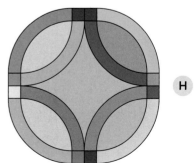

Quilt Construction

This quilt is assembled on the diagonal.

1. Follow the diagram to piece each diagonal row.

2. Sew the rows together, using the same method to find the center of each melon and center pieces. Press.

Finishing

Quilt, bind, and enjoy!

In the know.

• Only 1.4% of cotton grown in 2022 was certified organic.[6]

• The global textile and apparel industry had a retail value market of about $1.9 trillion in 2019. It is expected to reach up to $3.3 trillion by 2030.[7]

QUILT ASSEMBLY

6. *Textile Exchange. Organic Cotton Market Report (2022)*

7. *Bamaejuri Sohkhlet The Textile and Apparel Industry in South Korea (2021) Asia Internship Program*

Ombré Lone Star

FINISHED QUILT: 68½″ × 68½″

I SPENT SOME TIME CONTEMPLATING WHAT TO MAKE FROM THE REMAINING
They Got Married yardage. I wanted to make exciting quilts that would shine on their own. Enter
the Lone Star, a perennial favorite that's both dynamic and fun and easy to make.

The Lone Star and inner border were created using remaining fabric from *They Got Married*. I love this quilt because it shows the versatility of the ombré fabrics: bright and cheery in *They Got Married*, serious and earthy for this Lone Star.

I had to purchase the background fabric. I used backing fabric from my stash.

Materials

Yardages are based on 40˝-wide fabric.

If Starting with Leftovers OR Yardage

Fabric 1: 3½ yards assorted scraps for the Lone Star points and inner border

Fabric 2: 2¾ yards for background and border or 3½ yards to make *Ombré Lone Star* and the *Petal Pusher Pillow*

Backing: 4⅜ yards

Binding: ⅝ yard for bias binding

Batting: 76˝ × 76˝

Cutting

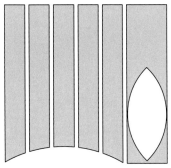

TIP

Lightly starch the fabric before cutting the strips to minimize stretch.

Fabric 1

Cut 96 strips 2½˝ wide across the width of the leftover *They Got Married* (page 46) fabric or yardage. Strips need to be a minimum of 20˝ long. You will have strips in varying lengths, anywhere from 20˝ to an entire WOF strip. Some strips may have wonky or curved ends from where a melon or center piece was cut. That is okay! Remember, we're using what we have in creative ways!

This is an example of how you can cut strips from fabric with a melon shape cut from it.

If Starting with Yardage

Cut 48 strips 2½˝ × WOF.

Fabric 2

Cut 4 squares 18˝ × 18˝.

Cut 1 square 25½˝ × 25½˝. Subcut into quarter-square triangles.

Cut 8 strips 4˝ × WOF for the border.

Construction

Seam allowances are ¼″ unless otherwise noted.

Make the Strip Sets

1. If starting with leftovers, assemble the strips into 16 groups of 6. If starting with yardage, assemble the strips into 8 groups of 6. Don't spend too much time worrying about color placement since all the pieces will ultimately blend together in the completed Lone Star.

2. If starting with leftovers, piece the strips in each group shortest to longest *if* possible with the right end offset 2½″ as shown. If starting with full WOF strips, piece the strips with the right ends offset 2½″. This ensures that there is fabric remaining when you cut on the diagonal. Press the seams open.

3. From each strip set, cut 3 2½″ wide strips at a 45° angle for a total of 48 strips. **A**

Make the Lone Star Center

1. Arrange the strips in 8 sets of 6 strips, following the diagram. **B**

2. Sew the strips together, making sure to offset the ends of each seam by ¼″ so that the seams match at the new seam line and the points line up.

3. Press the seams in the same direction on the back of each Lone Star section (i.e., all to the right or all to the left).

4. Sew 4 sections together to create the top half and bottom half of the Lone Star, stopping and backstitching at the inner points ¼″ from the edge.

5. Sew the halves together to make the Lone Star, also stopping and backstitching at the inner points. Continue to press seams in the same direction and furl the center of the Lone Star to minimize bulk. **C**

Make the Borders

MAKE THE INNER BORDER

Cut 1¾″-wide strips from the remaining strip sets. Sew pieces together to create 4 strips that each measure 1¾″ × 62″ long. Set aside. **D**

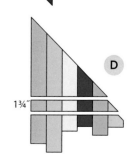

MAKE THE OUTER BORDER

Trim off the selvages and sew the 4″ × WOF outer border strips together to create one long 4″ strip. Cut 4 strips 4″ × 70″ long. Set aside.

Quilt Construction

1. Use Y-seams to sew the 18″ × 18″ background squares in the corners and the 25½″ × 25½″ quarter-square triangles to all 4 sides of the Lone Star to complete the center. Trim the corners and edges to measure 58½″ × 58½″ square.

2. Refer to How to Miter Corners (page 18) to sew the 1¾″ inner border to the Lone Star center.

3. Sew the 4″ outer border strips to the inner border. Miter the corners, press, and trim excess fabric.

Finishing

Quilt, bind, and enjoy.

In the know. According to the Environmental Protection Agency, textiles represented 5.8% of all municipal solid waste in 2018. American textile waste grew from 1,760,000 tons in 1960 to 17,030,000 tons in 2018, representing an 867% increase. There was a 33% increase in landfilled textiles between 1960 and 2018, growing from 1.7 million tons to 11.3 million tons.[8]

QUILT ASSEMBLY

---

8. United States Environmental Protection Agency. *Facts and Figures about Materials, Waste and Recycling* epa.gov

Petal Pusher Pillow

FINISHED PILLOW: 24″ × 24″

I WISH I COULD CREDIT THIS PILLOW TO EXCELLENT PLANNING, BUT IT'S MOSTLY a happy accident. I had a few melons I cut then didn't use from *They Got Married* and decided to use them in a pillow. Lucky for me, the size of the melons paired with the leftover fabric from *Ombré Lone Star* were the right size to make a Euro sham! Thus, a pillow was born.

If you didn't miscut any melon shapes, or need more, just cut some from the remaining ombré yardage.

Materials

Yardages are based on 40″-wide fabrics.

If Starting with Leftovers

10 miscut melons

3″ × 3″ square of ombré for flower center

Leftover background rectangle approximately 14½″ × 25½″

Leftover 28″ × WOF rectangle from *Ombré Lone Star* background

If Starting with Yardage

10 rectangles 5″ × 10½″

3″ × 3″ scrap for flower center

1¼ yards for pillow background

Additional Materials
FOR BOTH LEFTOVERS AND YARDAGE

Pillow insert: 24″ × 24″

Optional Double-sided fusible web (20″-wide): 1¼ yards (such as Steam-A-Seam or Lite Steam-A-Seam 2 by The Warm Company, or HeatnBond by Therm O Web; for fusing the appliqués.)

Optional: 2 buttons or a zipper

TIP
The pillow flaps more than cover the pillow insert, but if you'd like a slightly more tailored look, add a button or a zipper. If you use a zipper, adjust the sizes of the back pieces accordingly.

Cutting

If Starting with Leftovers

Cut a 3″ circle from the 3″ square using the Circle template (page 126).

Cut a 25½″ × 25½″ square and 2 rectangles 14½″ × 25½″ from the leftover background fabric.

If Starting with Yardage

Cut 10 petals from the 5″ × 10½″ rectangles using the Melon B template (page 124).

Cut a 3″ circle from the 3″ square using the Circle template (page 126).

Cut a 25½″ × 25½″ square and two rectangles 14½″ × 25½″ from the background fabric.

Construction

Seam allowances are ¼″ unless otherwise noted.

Appliqué the Melons

1. Use your method of choice to appliqué the melons and flower center to the front of the pillow.

TIP
Leaving 6⅝″ of space between each tip makes a perfect circle.

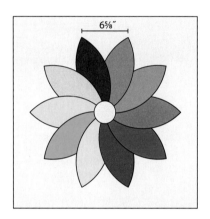

Prepare the Back

1. Hem 1 long edge of each 14½″ × 25½″ rectangle by folding and pressing ¼″ to the back.

2. Fold this edge again ⅜″. Press.

3. Stitch the hem with a straight stitch to secure the edge. **A**

4. If desired, you may place buttons and buttonholes along the finished edge to help keep the pillow closed. You can also use a zipper. If you choose to do this, you should zigzag or serge the edges to keep them from fraying before inserting the zipper between the back pieces.

Make the Pillow

This pillow is made using French seams. If preferred, you may use a serger to finish the pillow.

1. Place the pillow front right side down.

2. Place the 14½″ × 25½″ pillow backs on the pillow front, right side up and matching the raw edges. The finished hems of the pillow backs will overlap slightly in the center.

3. Sew a ¼″ seam allowance around the entire pillow. **B**

4. Trim seam to ⅛″.

5. Turn pillow wrong side out, gently pushing the corners out, and press. Sew around the entire pillow with a ¼″ seam allowance. **C**

6. Turn pillowcase right side out and press.

7. Place pillow insert into pillowcase and enjoy!

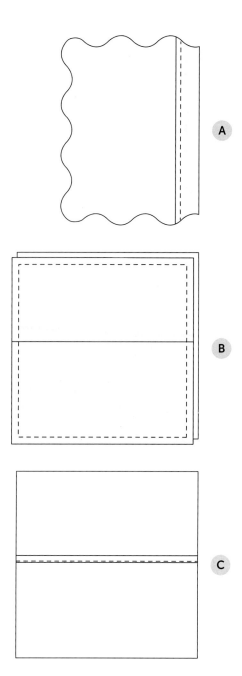

No Fences Table Runner

FINISHED BLOCK: 15″ × 15″ • FINISHED TABLE RUNNER: 15″ × 90″

I ADORE THIS TABLE RUNNER! IN FACT, AS SOON AS WE HAD THE FINAL photography for the book, I put it on my dining room table. It makes me smile daily. This table runner was made with the leftover triangle-shaped strip-pieced sets from *Ombré Lone Star*. The strip sets work together to create large, bold quarter-square triangle blocks.

I used backing fabric from my stash and scrap batting.

Materials

Yardages are based on 40″-wide fabrics.

If Starting with Leftovers

Leftover strip-pieced triangles sections from *Ombré Lone Star* points

If Starting with Yardage

1⅞ yards of assorted scraps

Additional Materials

FOR BOTH LEFTOVERS AND YARDAGE

Backing: 15½″ × 90½″

Batting: 15½″ × 90½″

TIP

This table runner was finished with an envelope method. If you would like to quilt it as a sandwich, you will need 20″ × 95″ for the backing and batting and ½ yard for binding.

Cutting

If Starting with Yardage

Cut 24 strips 2½″ × WOF.

Construction

Seam allowances are ¼″ unless otherwise noted.

If Starting with Leftovers

MAKE THE QUARTER-SQUARES

After cutting the Lone Star strips, striped triangles pieces will remain. Trim the triangles to create the Quarter-Squares for the table runner.

The 90-degree triangles need to measure 11½″ × 11½″ along the short sides ; *however*, your triangles may be slightly smaller or larger. Measure all triangles to find the smallest one, then either trim all the pieces to that size *or* add pieces to make them larger.

This triangle was large enough to cut out a quarter-square piece. **A**

If you don't have enough triangles or they are too small, you can combine leftovers.

These two triangles are both too small, but if you combine the triangles, you can make a quarter-square triangle that is the correct size. **B–C**

When you combine the 2 halves you can create a quarter-square triangle that is the correct size. **D**

You need 24 quarter-square triangles to complete this table runner.

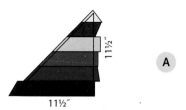

A

B

Use the top 4 pieces of this triangle.

C

Use the bottom 2 pieces of this triangle.

D

If Starting with Yardage

1. Sort the 2½″ strips into 4 sets of 6 strips.

2. Sew each set of strips together along the long edges. Press the seams open. **E**

3. Cut 3 squares 11½″ × 11½″ each from each strip set. **F**

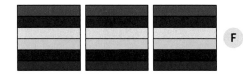

4. Cut each square into half-square triangles. Make sure you cut all the half-square triangles in the *same* direction (i.e., from lower left to top right, etc.). **G**

Make the Table Runner

Seam allowances are ¼″ unless otherwise noted.

1. Sew 4 triangles together to create a 15½″ × 15½″ block. Press.

2. Repeat Step 1 to make 6 blocks. **H**

3. Arrange the blocks in a row and sew together.

4. Layer right sides together with the backing and add the batting. Secure the edges with clips or pins. Sew around all 4 edges, leaving a 4″ opening to turn.

5. Clip the corners and turn right side out, gently poke the corners out, and press. Whipstitch the opening closed.

6. Quilt and enjoy!

Ingenious Batting and Quilt Back Substitutes

There are a lot of easy-to-find items you can use as a substitute for batting and quilt backing. The substrates mentioned below are all 100% natural fibers and don't include any synthetic materials, which release microplastics when washed. Be sure to prewash anything listed to allow it to shrink before using it in a quilt.

- Flannel yardage or flannel sheets

- Wool or wool blankets

- Pieced cotton or wool batting

- An old cotton quilt or cotton blanket

- Ticking

You can make a summer quilt by omitting the batting—perfect for warm weather!

Dinner Belle

FINISHED NAPKIN: 11½″ × 11½″

I DECIDED IF I WAS MAKING A TABLE RUNNER, I SHOULD HAVE DINNER NAPKINS to go with it! This makes six napkins that are on the smaller side, but you can make yours larger if desired.

TIP

Construction is the same if you want larger napkins, but the larger square *must* be 4″ larger than the smaller square (i.e., 18″ × 18″ for the large square and 14″ × 14″ for the smaller square to make a 15½″ × 15½″ finished napkin).

Materials

Yardages are based on 40″-wide fabric.

If Starting with Leftovers

6 squares 10″ × 10″ of assorted leftovers for the napkin center

6 squares 14″ × 14″ of assorted leftovers for the outer border

If Starting with Yardage

Fabric 1: ¾ yard for the napkin center

Fabric 2: 1⅜ yards for the outer border

Cutting

You can use any combination of fabrics for these dinner napkins.

Napkin Center

Cut 6 squares 10″ × 10″.

Contrasting Outer Border

Cut 6 squares 14″ × 14″.

Construction

Seam allowances are ¼″ unless otherwise noted.

1. Mark the center of each side of all squares with a pin or by pressing.

2. Place a smaller square on top of a larger square, right sides together. Pin the centers together and place pins ¼″ from each corner of the smaller square. **A**

3. Sew between the ¼″ marks. Backstitch to lock seams in place. **B**

4. Continue around all 4 sides. Leave a 3″ opening in the middle of one side so you can turn the napkin right side out. **C**

5. Fold the smaller square diagonally onto itself, allowing the tail of the larger napkin to sit off to the side. **D**

6. With the ruler line at the fold, mark a diagonal line from the fold to the end of the stitching to mark the miter. Pin the corner. **E–F**

7. Sew on the line and trim the tail. **G**

8. Turn napkin right side out and press. Edgestitch along the inner seam to complete. **H**

9. Repeat Steps 2–8 to make 6 napkins. Enjoy!

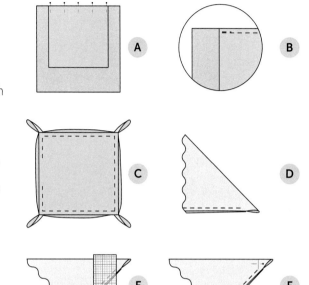

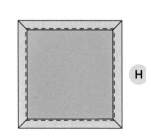

Sip Back

FINISHED NAPKIN: 5˝ × 5˝

NATURALLY, DINNER NAPKINS LED TO A SET OF SIX COCKTAIL NAPKINS.

Materials

Yardages are based on 40˝-wide fabric.

If Starting with Leftovers

12 squares 5˝ × 5˝ from assorted leftover fabric from *They Got Married*

If Starting with Yardage

⅓ yard

Cutting

Cut 12 squares 5˝ × 5˝ from fabric.

Construction

Seam allowances are ¼˝ unless otherwise noted.

1. Place 2 squares *wrong sides together* and sew ¼˝ around the edges.

2. Repeat Step 1 to make 6 napkins.

3. Gently fray the edges using a straight pin, stiletto, or your fingers.

4. Enjoy!

In the know. Turkey is one of the largest producers of organic cotton in the Middle East. The country has been growing and manufacturing organic cotton products since the 1980s.[9]

9. Textile Exchange. Organic Cotton Market Report (2022)

Gather Round

FINISHED PLACE MAT: 12″ × 18″

THESE SIX PLACE MATS ARE PIECED USING LEFTOVER OMBRÉ LONE STAR STRIPS
and leftover yardage from *They Got Married*. I mixed leftover pieces to create an overall cohesive
look to go with the table runner, napkins, and cocktail napkins. Together, the look is fun and
festive!

I used backing fabric and scrap batting from my stash.

Materials

Yardages are based on 40″-wide fabric.

If Starting with Leftovers

Leftover yardage from *They Got Married*

Leftover 2½″ strips from *Ombré Lone Star*

If Starting with Yardage

Yardages are based on 40″ wide fabric.

For large rectangle: ⅔ yard

For small rectangle: ⅓ yard

For accent strip: ½ yard assorted scraps

Additional Materials FOR BOTH LEFTOVERS AND YARDAGE

Backing: 1¼ yards

Batting: 1 package (crib size) for the set of 6

TIP

These place mats were finished with an envelope method. If you would like to quilt the place mats as a sandwich and bind, you will need an additional ¾ yard for bias binding. You will also need a 17″ × 23″ rectangle of batting for each place mat.

Cutting

If Starting with Leftovers

Remaining yardage will vary depending on how you cut the fabric in earlier projects, so there's some improv involved making these. The rectangular panels on each side of the accent strip will measure differently for each place mat. Each place mat finishes at 12″ × 18″, and the finished width of the accent strip is 2″, so the width of the left and right panels must total 16″ before adding ¼″ seam allowances to each side. All pieces must be 12½″ high.

For example, if you have a 5½″ × 12½″ leftover rectangle to use for a place mat (16 − 5 = 11), you will need to cut an 11½″ × 12½″ rectangle to make an 18″-wide place mat (5½″ + 2½″ + 11½″ − seam allowances = 18″).

Cut two rectangles of fabric for each place mat.

TIP

If you are making place mats from leftover fabric, the left and right panels will vary in size. Directions to make the place mats from new yardage assumes the left and right panels are the same.

If Starting with Yardage

LARGE SQUARES
Cut 6 squares 12½″ × 12½″.

SMALL RECTANGLES
Cut 6 rectangles 4½″ × 12½″.

ACCENT STRIPS
Cut 1 strip 2½″ × WOF from 6 fabrics.

BACKING
Cut 6 rectangles 12½″ × 18½.″

BATTING
Cut 6 rectangles 12½″ × 18½.″

Construction

Seam allowances are ¼″ unless otherwise noted.

Make the Accent Piece

1. Sew the 2½″ strips together. **A**

2. Cut 6 strips 2½″ each at a 45° angle from the strip set. **B**

3. Trim each strip to 2½″ × 12½″.

Make the Place Mats

1. Sew the rectangles to both sides of the accent strip. Press. **C**

2. Layer the top and backing right sides together with the batting. Secure the edges with clips or pins.

3. Sew around all 4 edges, leaving a 4″ opening to turn.

4. Clip the corners and turn right side out. Gently poke corners out and press. Whipstitch the opening closed.

5. Quilt and enjoy!

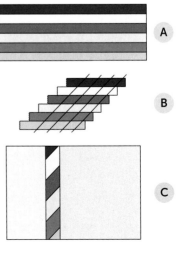

Lavender for Days

FINISHED BLOCK: 17″ × 17″ • FINISHED QUILT: 63½″ × 63½″

WHAT DO YOU DO WITH A RANDOM ASSORTMENT OF FABRIC THAT DOESN'T FIT TOGETHER? You cut down the pieces and **make** them fit together. Cutting larger pieces of fabric into smaller squares that will sew together proportionally is an easy way to build an entire quilt or blocks. I cut my squares to finish at 6″, 3,″ and 1″ but if you want the blocks larger you can cut squares to finish at 8″, 4,″ and 2″ or any other combination of sizes you like.

The fabric that borders the blocks, the lavender background, and the backing fabric were all from my stash.

Materials

If Starting with Leftovers

9 squares 6½″ × 6½″

72 squares 3½″ × 3½″

360 squares 2″ × 2″

168 squares 1½″ × 1½″

1″ strips in a variety of lengths

If Starting with Yardage

Fabric 1: 2⅔ yards assorted fabrics to make the center blocks

Additional Materials
FOR BOTH LEFTOVERS AND YARDAGE

Fabric 2: ⅞ yard for block frames

Fabric 3: 1⅜ yards for sashing and borders

Backing: 4⅛ yards

Binding: ½ yard

Batting: 72″ × 72″

Cutting

If Starting with Yardage

FABRIC 1

Cut 9 squares 6½″ × 6½″.

Cut 72 squares 3½″ × 3½″.

Cut 360 squares 2″ × 2″.

Cut 168 squares 1½″ × 1½″.

Cut any remaining leftovers into 1″-wide strips with varying lengths.

Additional Yardage

FABRIC 2

Cut 18 strips 1½″ × WOF. Subcut each strip into:

    1 rectangle 1½″ × 17½″

    1 rectangle 1½″ × 15½″

FABRIC 3

Cut 3 strips 3½″ × WOF. Subcut 6 rectangles 3½″ × 17½″.

Cut 9 strips 3½″ × WOF. Remove selvage edges and with right sides together sew strips end to end, plus add a leftover 3½″ × 5″ rectangle from the previous step. Subcut 2 strips 3½″ × 63½″ and 4 strips 3½″ × 57½″.

Construction

Seam allowances are ¼″ unless otherwise noted.

Make Block A

Sew 6 blocks together as follows.

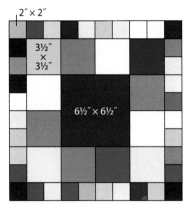

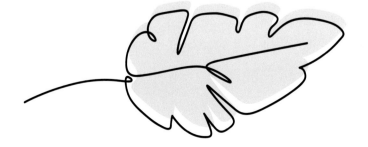

Make Block B

MAKE THE 1″ BLOCK INNER BORDER

1. Sew the 1″ strips end to end to make the inner block border.

2. Cut 6 rectangles 1″ × 12½″ and 6 rectangles 1″ × 13½″.

Sew 3 blocks together as follows, adding the 1″ block inner borders. **A**

Add the Block Frames

1. Sew a 1½″ × 15½″ rectangle to two opposite sides of each block. Press.

2. Sew a 1½″ × 17½″ rectangle to the remaining two sides of each block. Press. **B**

Make the Quilt

1. Arrange the blocks in 3 rows of 3 blocks.

2. Sew 2 sashing strips 3½″ × 17½″ between 3 blocks to create a row. Repeat for remaining 2 rows. **C**

3. Sew the 3½″ × 57½″ strips between the rows and to the top and bottom.

4. Sew 3½″ × 63½″ strip to each side.

5. Quilt, bind, and enjoy!

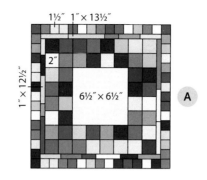

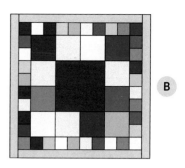

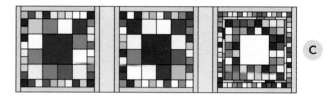

QUILT ASSEMBLY

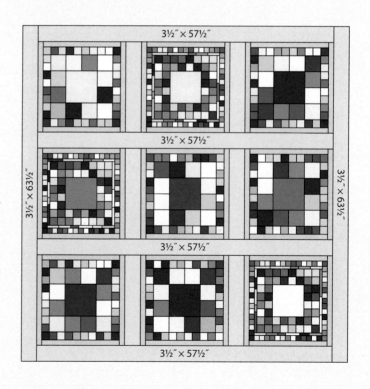

Amelia's Rainbow

FINISHED QUILT: 28½″ × 30½″

THE ARCS FROM *THEY GOT MARRIED* WERE CREATED FROM VIBRANT FLORAL
fabrics. After cutting out the arcs, the dominant shape remaining in the scrap was a triangle.
After cutting out the remaining triangles in a variety of sizes, I decided to put them together and
create a vivid floral, rainbow quilt.

Rarely does a quilt I make have a name before it's finished. Usually, the name comes to me while I'm quilting it. Sometimes after. This quilt was different. The day I finished piecing this quilt top, a friend's dog suddenly passed away. Heartbroken for her, knowing how hard it is to have a pup cross the Rainbow Bridge unexpectedly, I named this in honor of sweet Amelia, a foster fail who was lucky enough to live out her days in a wonderfully loving home.

The backing, batting, and binding were all from my stash.

Materials

Yardages are based on 40″-wide fabrics.

If Starting with Leftovers

420 half-square triangles from *They Got Married* arcs

If Starting with Yardage

1½ yards assorted scraps

Additional Materials

FOR BOTH LEFTOVERS AND YARDAGE

Backing: 1 yard

Binding: ½ yard

Batting: 33″ × 35″

Cutting

Refer to Basic Block Construction (page 16) for half-square triangle instructions.

If Starting with Leftovers

Cut the leftover pieces from the floral arcs, see Assorted Florals (page 47) into triangles. You should be able to get 3 half-square triangles 3″ each from the center half-melon, a 4¼″ to 4½″ half-square triangle from one side and 2 half-square triangles 1⅞″ each from the remaining sides (1⅞″ half-square triangles will be used in

the zipper pouches). Don't worry if you get more or fewer half-square triangles from the leftover floral arcs. Cut whatever you can.

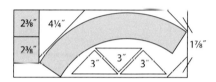

Cut any 4¼″ and 4½″ half-square triangles in half.

If Starting with Yardage

Cut 210 squares 3″ × 3″. Subcut into half-square triangles.

Construction

Seam allowances are ¼″ unless otherwise noted.

Arrange the Half-Square Triangles and Make Blocks

1. Arrange the 3″ and 4¼″– 4½″ half-square triangles on a design wall. Some half-square triangles will be slightly larger than others because of how they were cut. That's okay! The squares will all get trimmed down to the same size in Step 3.

This quilt has 15 rows, each with 14 blocks, but your quilt layout

may differ depending on color placement and how many half-square triangle units you have.

2. Sew the half-square triangles together.

3. Press and trim to 2½″ × 2½″ squares.

Make the Quilt

1. Sew the half-square triangle blocks into rows and press.

2. Sew the rows together and press.

3. Quilt, bind, and enjoy!

QUILT ASSEMBLY

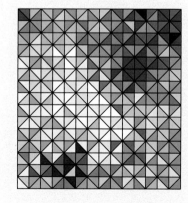

Getting Zippy with It

FINISHED POUCHES: 9″ × 3″, 12″ × 9″, and 15″ × 9″

THESE ZIPPER POUCHES WERE MADE AS A SET USING ALL THE LEFTOVER FABRICS.
Combining ombré and floral scraps in a variety of sizes as well as the leftover mitered border pieces from the Lone Star made fun and interesting pouches.

Any scraps of ombré remaining were cut into 1½″ × 1½″ squares and the leftover floral border fabric from *Lavender for Days* was also cut down into 1½″ × 1½″ squares.

Materials

Yardages are based on 40"-wide fabrics.

You will have an assortment of half-square triangles from *Amelia's Rainbow* (page 69) and block centers from the *They Got Married Quilt* (page 46). Make as many half-square triangles from those pieces as you can before you make the zipper pouches.

If Starting with Leftovers

SMALL ZIPPER POUCH

39 squares and half-square triangles 1½" × 1½" from leftover ombré and *Amelia's Rainbow*

6 half-square triangles 2½" × 2½" from leftover ombré and *Amelia's Rainbow*

2 rectangles of 3½" × 9½" sashing strips from *Lavender for Days* for lining

MEDIUM ZIPPER POUCH

6 rectangles 1" × 5" of assorted ombré scraps

28 half-square triangles 1½" × 1½" from leftover *Amelia's Rainbow*

48 half-square triangles 2½" × 2½" from leftover *Amelia's Rainbow*

2 rectangles 1¾" × 5½" from leftover *Ombré Lone Star*

1 rectangle 2" × 6" from leftover *Ombré Lone Star*

2 rectangles 2" × 10½" from leftover *Ombré Lone Star*

6 angled ends from border strips from leftover *Ombré Lone Star*

⅜ yard for lining and pockets*

LARGE ZIPPER POUCH

270 squares and half-square triangles 1½" × 1½" from leftover ombré and *Amelia's Rainbow*

1 rectangle 2½" × 9" for handle (leftover from *Ombré Lone Star* or can be cut from lining and pocket yardage)

½ yard for lining, pockets, and handle *

*If you are making both the medium and large pouches, ⅝ yard is enough to cut the linings, pockets, and handles for both.

If Starting with Yardage

SMALL ZIPPER POUCH

⅛ yard

MEDIUM ZIPPER POUCH

½ yard

LARGE ZIPPER POUCH

⅝ yard

Additional Materials
FOR BOTH LEFTOVERS AND YARDAGE

9" zipper for small pouch

12" zipper for medium pouch

15" zipper for large pouch

Cutting

If Starting with Leftovers

Cut leftover half-melon-like shapes into 2 or 3 squares and 2 half-square triangles. Squares should be 1½" × 1½" but sizes may vary if you miscut. Trim the 2 outside pieces to the largest triangle you can create.

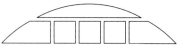

How to cut half-melons into smaller pieces

Lining fabric

If cutting both the medium and large pouches, use diagram. Otherwise see list below.

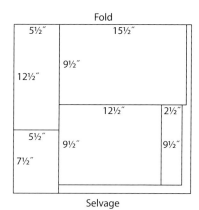

MEDIUM ZIPPER POUCH

Cut 2 rectangles 9½" × 12½" for lining.

Cut 2 rectangles 5½" × 12½" for pocket.

LARGE ZIPPER POUCH

Cut 2 rectangles 9½" × 15½" for lining.

Cut 2 rectangles 5½" × 7½" for pocket.

Cut 1 rectangle 2½" × 9½" for handle (if not cut from scraps before.)

If Starting with Yardage

SMALL ZIPPER POUCH

Cut 4 rectangles 3½″ × 9½″.

MEDIUM ZIPPER POUCH

Cut 4 rectangles 9½″ × 12½″.

Cut 2 rectangles 5½″ × 12½″ for pocket.

LARGE ZIPPER POUCH

Cut 4 rectangles 9½″ × 15½″.

Cut 2 rectangles 5½″ × 7½″ for pocket.

Cut 1 rectangle 2½″ × 9½″ for handle.

Construction

Seam allowances are ¼″ unless otherwise noted.

How to make half-square triangles from leftovers

1. Pair similarly sized triangles. **A**

2. Draw a 45° line across the back of one triangle. Be sure to leave a ¼″ seam allowance. **B**

3. Sew triangles together. Trim a ¼″ seam allowance. **C**

4. Press half-square triangles and trim.

5. Repeat Steps 2–4 to make 54 squares 2½″ × 2½″ and 337 squares 1½″ × 1½″. **D**

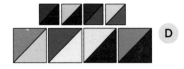

Small Zipper Pouch

1. Arrange 27 squares 1½″ × 1½″ in a 9 × 3 grid for one side of the pouch. **E**

2. Sew the pieces together into rows and press in opposite directions, and then sew the rows together. Press the seams open.

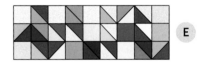

3. Arrange 6 half-square triangles 2½″ × 2½″ and 12 squares as shown for the second side. **F**

4. Sew the 2½″ × 2½″ half-square triangles together and press. Trim this unit to 5½″ × 3½″.

5. Sew the 1½″ × 1½″ squares into units and add to the Step 4 unit.

6. Proceed to Finishing the Zipper Pouches (page 74).

Medium Zipper Pouch

1. Arrange a 1″ × 5″ rectangle between 2 triangles cut from the 4″ *Ombré Lone Star* border. **G**

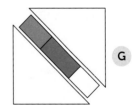

2. Sew the strips between 2 triangles. Press and trim to 3″ × 3″. **H**

3. Repeat Steps 1 and 2 to make 6 blocks.

4. Arrange and sew the 6 blocks into 2 rows of 3.

5. Sew a 1¾″ × 5½″ rectangle to each end of the squares. Press.

6. Sew a 2″ × 10½″ rectangle to the remaining two sides. Press.

7. Sew a row of 1½″ × 1½″ half-square triangles around 3 sides of the pouch cover. Press. **I**

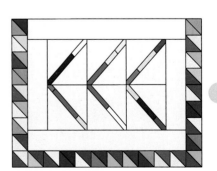

8. For the back of the pouch, arrange and sew the 2½″ × 2½″ half-square triangles into 6 rows of 8. Sew into rows and press in opposite directions. Sew the rows together and press the seams open. **J**

9. Fold the 2″ × 6″ rectangle in half lengthwise and stitch together along the long edge. Turn right side out and press to make the handle. Fold in half and pin or thread baste to one side of the zipper pouch, about 1½″ from the top edge.

10. Proceed to Finishing the Zipper Pouches.

Large Zipper Pouch

1. Arrange 135 half-square triangles and squares 1½″ × 1½″ to make the front cover of the large zipper pouch according to diagram. **K**

2. Sew the blocks together into rows and press each row opposite.

3. Sew the rows together and press the seams open.

4. Repeat Steps 1–3 for the back of the zipper pouch.

5. Fold the 2½″ × 9″ rectangle in half lengthwise, right sides together, and sew together along the long edge. Turn right side out and press to make the handle. Pin or thread baste to one side of the zipper pouch, about 1½″ from the top edge.

6. Proceed to Finishing the Zipper Pouches.

Finishing the Zipper Pouches
Attach the Zipper

1. Mark the center of the zipper and the center of the front side of the zipper pouch. Place the zipper, right sides together, on top of the pouch exterior, matching the centers and edges. Use a zipper foot to sew the zipper to the pouch. **L**

2. Repeat Step 1 on the other side of the pouch.

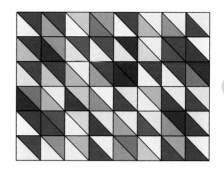

J

K

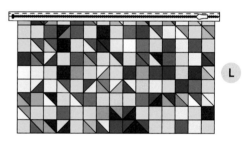

L

3. Place the right side of the lining fabric over the zipper and matching the edge. Use a zipper foot to sew the lining to the zipper. Press the lining and exterior away from the zipper. **M**

4. Repeat Step 3 for the other side of the pouch.

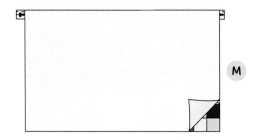

5. Topstitch the zipper pouch cover and lining to the zipper to prevent the fabric from getting stuck in the zipper when you open and close the pouch. **N**

Add the Pockets

MEDIUM ZIPPER POUCH

1. Place the 5½″ × 12½″ pocket rectangles right sides together and sew along one 12½″ side.

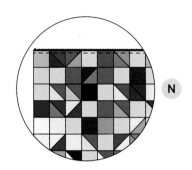

2. Turn right side out, press, and edgestitch along the sewn edge.

3. Place the pocket along one 12½″ side of the lining fabric, matching the lower edges. Pin or thread baste into place.

LARGE ZIPPER POUCH

1. Use the 5½″ × 7½″ pocket pieces for the large pouch. Press a ¼″ toward the wrong side of the fabric along each edge, then press ⅜″ down again.

2. Place each pocket onto the lining, making sure the opening is facing the top of the pouch, and edgestitch into place.

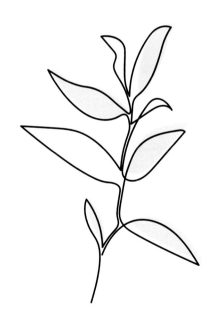

Completing the Zipper Pouches

1. Open the zipper halfway.

2. Fold the zipper pouch in half so the lining pieces are right sides together and the front and back pieces are right sides together. Make sure you fold the zipper pieces toward the lining.

3. Sew front and back of the zipper pouch together. Clip the corners.

4. Turn right side out. Press.

5. Enjoy!

Checkerboard Trivet

FINISHED TRIVET: 8½″ × 6¾″

I NEVER SEEM TO HAVE ENOUGH TRIVETS, ESPECIALLY WHEN WE HAVE GUESTS
for dinner, so when I was down to the very last pieces of ombré fabric, it occurred to me that I
really needed another trivet for my outdoor oasis.

Created with the last of the *They Got Married* scraps, this fun project is handy to have and easy
to make.

Materials

Yardages are based on 40˝-wide fabrics.

If Starting with Leftovers

Leftover *Ombré Lone Star* inner border strips

3 Lone Star point strip leftovers

Assorted scraps from *Getting Zippy with It* pouch linings

If Starting with Yardage

Yardages are based on 40˝ wide fabric.

20 rectangles 1¾˝ × 2½˝

Binding: 2˝ × WOF

Additional Materials
FOR BOTH LEFTOVERS AND YARDAGE

Batting *or* Insulated Batting: 9˝ × 11˝

Construction

Seam allowances are ¼˝ unless otherwise noted.

Make the Top of the Trivet

IF STARTING WITH LEFTOVERS

1. Carefully separate the inner border to make 5 strips, each with 4 pieces. Each strip should measure 1¾˝ × 8½˝ unfinished. **A, B**

2. Sew the rows together and press. **C**

IF STARTING WITH YARDAGE

1. Sew 4 rectangles together to create a 1¾˝ × 8½˝ strip. Repeat to make a total of 5 strips. **B**

2. Sew rows together and press. **C**

Make the Back of the Trivet

A handful of very incohesive, oddly sized fabric remained after I finished the trivet top. I decided to sew the pieces together to create a mishmash back.

Piece oddly sized leftovers to create a back for the trivet. **D**

Trivet Construction

1. Layer trivet top, batting, and backing. Quilt as desired.

2. Bind using leftover bias strips from the Lone Star or other binding of choice.

3. Enjoy!

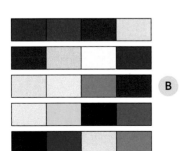

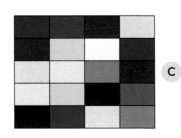

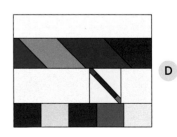

Make Your Own Fabric

One great way to use fabric scraps is to make new fabric. Sew strips together by color to create fabric. You can subcut the fabric into squares, half-square triangles, or other shapes to use as blocks, coping strips, sashing, and more!

You can also sew assorted shapes, strips, and scraps together to create an improv piece, or an improv-style fabric for quilts.

The blocks in the center of this quilt were made entirely from fabric scraps.

Close-up of quilt blocks

Fringeworthy

FINISHED SIZE: varies

I LOVE A GOOD PARTY AND FESTIVE DECOR, BUT IF I'M HONEST, I DON'T HAVE much. Festive fringe, you say? Great idea! This party fringe is an excellent way to put leftover strips to good use and bring some cheer. It's easy to do with any strips and you can group pieces by color or theme to create a fringe that coordinates with any holiday or party. So fun!

Bonus: now this fringe permanently hangs in my studio and adds a little cheer to my space.

Materials

Leftover strips of fabric

1¼ yards of twine or jute

Construction

1. Fold any leftover strips in half and arrange by size on the floor, with the longest strips in the middle and the shortest strips on the ends. **A**

2. Starting in the middle, gently knot a fabric strip around the twine with a lark's head knot. **B–C**

3. Work out to each end until all scraps have been tied to the twine. **D**

4. Hang between two columns, pillars, or trees or on a wall to create a fun, festive party backdrop!

5. Enjoy!

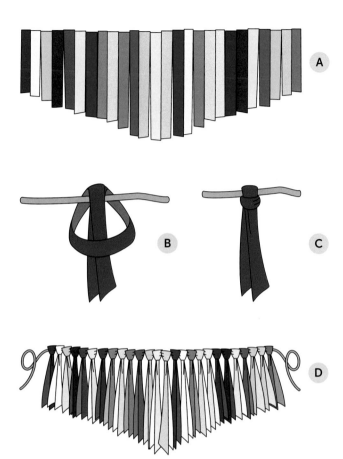

⟨⟨ He who knows what sweets and virtues are in the ground, the waters, the plants, the heavens, and how to come at these enchantments, is the rich and royal man." **RALPH WALDO EMERSON**

Poppies in Tuscany

FINISHED BLOCKS: 9˝ × 9˝, 4½˝ × 9˝, and 4½˝ × 4½˝ • FINISHED QUILT: 86˝ × 86˝

Quilted by Cheryl Ashley-Serafine

WHILE WRITING THIS MANUSCRIPT, I WAS FORTUNATE ENOUGH TO SPEND TIME in Italy celebrating a myriad of family milestones. I originally planned to make this quilt in a different color story but returned from my trip inspired by all the yellow, gold, and orange poppies! They are everywhere!

All the yellow and gold fabrics play together nicely, and the orange stars give this quilt a nice pop!

I had to purchase the white background fabric.

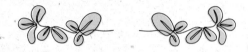

Materials

Yardages are based on 40″-wide fabrics.

Fabric 1: ½ yard orange

Fabric 2: 3¾ yards background fabric

Fabric 3: 6¼ yards assorted yellow

Backing: 8 yards

Binding: ¾ yard

Batting: 94″ × 94″

Cutting

Refer to Basic Block Construction (page 16) for half-square triangle and quarter-square triangle instructions.

Fabric 1

Cut 1 strip 3½″ × WOF. Subcut 6 squares 3½″ × 3½″; subcut into half-square triangles.

Cut 2 strips 3¼″ × WOF. Subcut 12 strips 3¼″ × 5⅞″; then subcut:

6 rectangles into half-rectangle triangles, top left to bottom right **A**

6 rectangles into half-rectangle triangles, top right to bottom left **B**

Fabric 2

Cut 6 strips 5⅞″ × WOF. Subcut 36 squares 5⅞″ × 5⅞″; then subcut into quarter-square triangles.

Cut 14 strips 4½″ × WOF. Subcut 84 diamonds using Template A (page 123).

Cut 5 strips 3¾″ × WOF. Subcut 49 squares 3¾″ × 3¾″.

Fabric 3

Cut 11 strips 5½″ × WOF. Subcut 72 squares 5½″ × 5½″; the subcut into half-square triangles.

Cut 5 strips 5″ × WOF. Subcut 36 squares 5″ × 5″.

Cut 9 strips 3½″ × WOF. Subcut 92 squares 3½″ × 3½″; subcut into half-square triangles.

Cut 26 strips 3¼″ × WOF. Subcut 156 rectangles 3¼″ × 5⅞″; then subcut:

78 rectangles into half-rectangle triangles, top left to bottom right **A**

78 rectangles into half-rectangle triangles, top right to bottom left **B**

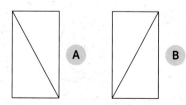

Make the Blocks

Refer to Basic Block Construction (page 16) for square-in-a-square instructions.

Make the Small Square-in-a-Square Blocks

1. Sew 4 half-square triangles 3½″ × 3½″ to a square 3¾″ × 3¾″.

2. Trim blocks to 5″ × 5″ square.

3. Repeat Steps 1 and 2 to make 46 blocks with a variety of yellow and background fabrics and 3 blocks with a background square and orange Fabric 1 triangles. **A**

Make the Large Square-in-a-Square-in-a-Square Blocks

1. Sew 4 quarter-square triangles 5⅞″ × 5⅞″ to a 5″ × 5″ center square.

2. Trim to 6⅞″ × 6⅞″.

3. Add the 4 half-square triangles 5½″ × 5½″.

4. Trim block to 9½″ × 9½″ square. **B**

5. Repeat Steps 1–4 to make 36 blocks.

Make the Diamond in a Square Blocks

1. Sew a half-rectangle triangle to one side of a diamond. Match the point at the top of the diamond to the lower point on the half-rectangle triangle. Press. **C**

2. Repeat Step 1 to add half-rectangle triangles to the remaining sides of the diamond. **D–E**

3. Press and trim to 5″ × 9½″.

4. Repeat Steps 1–3 to make 30 background and yellow blocks and 12 background and orange blocks as shown in the assembly diagram.

Quilt Assembly

1. Arrange the blocks according to the diagram below.

2. Sew each row. Press.

3. Sew the rows together. Press.

4. Quilt, bind, and enjoy!

  A B C D 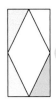 E

QUILT ASSEMBLY

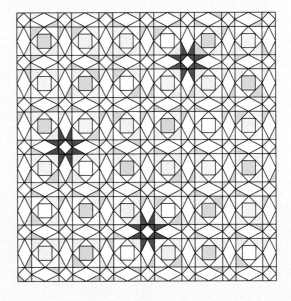

Rays of Sunshine

FINISHED QUILT: 32¼″ × 36¾″

THIS SMALL QUILT WAS SURPRISINGLY CHALLENGING TO CREATE BECAUSE I HAD to figure out how to put a collection of irregularly shaped triangles together in a cohesive piece. To my frustration and dismay, several larger iterations of this quilt didn't come together, so I decided to make the piece smaller. The angled background fabrics paired with leftover strips from *Poppies in Tuscany* created a base. Grouping these pieces together creates order and logic, and makes sense of irregular shapes, working together to create a cohesive piece.

The sashing, border, and binding were all from my stash. The inner border was made from leftover binding yardage from *Poppies in Tuscany*.

Materials

Yardages are based on 40″-wide fabrics.

If Starting with Leftovers

28 light background triangles, leftover from *Poppies in Tuscany*

26 yellow leftover rectangles at least 1⅝″ × 6¾″

2 orange rectangles 3¼″ × 6¾″, and 8″ × WOF

¼ yard light background strip

Inner Border: 3½″ × WOF orange leftover from *Poppies in Tuscany*

If Starting with Yardage

Light background: ⅝ yard

Orange: ¼ yard for blocks and inner border

Yellow: ⅓ yard

Additional Materials FOR BOTH LEFTOVERS AND YARDAGE

Sashing: ½ yard

Outer Border: ½ yard

Backing: 1 yard

Batting: 41″ × 45″

Binding: ⅓ yard for straight grain binding

Cutting

From Leftovers

Cut 2 orange 3¼″ × 6¾″ strips in half to make 4 strips 1⅝″ × 6¾″.

Cut 16 squares 4½″ × 4½″ from the ¼ yard light background fabric. Subcut into half-square triangles.

Cut 26 yellow strips 1⅝″ × 6¾″.

From Yardage

ORANGE FABRIC:

Cut 1 strip 1⅝″ × WOF. Subcut 4 strips 1⅝″ × 6¾″. Set remainder aside for inner border.

YELLOW FABRIC:

Cut 6 strips 1⅝″ × WOF. Subcut 26 strips 1⅝″ × 6¾″.

LIGHT BACKGROUND FABRIC:

Cut 4 strips 4½″ × WOF. Subcut 30 squares 4½″ × 4½,″ then subcut into half-square triangles.

Sashing

Cut 9 strips 1½″ × WOF. Subcut into:

  2 strips 1½″ × 28½″

  7 strips 1½″ × 22″

  24 strips 1½″ × 4″

Inner Border

FROM LEFTOVERS OR NEW YARDAGE:

Cut 3 strips 1⅛″ × WOF.

Outer Border

Cut 3 strips 4″ × WOF.

Construction

Seam allowances are ¼˝ unless otherwise noted.

Make the Blocks

1. Sew a 1⅝˝ × 6¾˝ rectangle between leftover and/or half-square triangles. Press. **A**

2. Trim to 4˝ × 4˝ square. Repeat to make 30 blocks. **B**

Attach the Sashing

1. Arrange the blocks in 6 rows of 5 blocks.

2. Sew a 1½˝ × 4˝ sashing strip between the blocks. Repeat for each row.

3. Sew a 1½˝ × 22˝ sashing strip between each row and to the top and bottom.

4. Sew a 1½˝ × 28½˝ sashing strip to each side.

Attach the Inner Border

1. Trim off selvage and sew the 3 strips 1⅛˝ × WOF together end to end.

2. Cut 2 strips 1⅛˝ × 24˝ and 2 strips 1⅛˝ × 29¾˝.

3. Sew the 1⅛˝ × 24˝ strips to the top and bottom of the quilt.

4. Sew the 1⅛˝ × 29¾˝ strips to the sides of the quilt.

Attach the Outer Border

1. Trim off the selvages and sew 3 strips 4˝ × WOF strips together end to end.

2. Cut 2 strips 4˝ × 25¼˝ and 2 strips 4˝ × 36¾˝.

3. Sew a 4˝ × 25¼˝ strip to the top and bottom of the quilt.

4. Sew a 4˝ × 36¾˝ strip to the sides of the quilt.

Finishing

Quilt, bind, and enjoy!

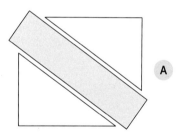

A

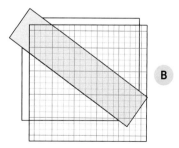

B

QUILT ASSEMBLY

Hello Sunshine

FINISHED TOWELS: 20″ × 20″

I ORIGINALLY MADE THE HALF-SQUARE TRIANGLE TOWEL AS A WALL HANGING
but decided to turn it into a tea towel when the assortment of pieces I had remaining wasn't
enough for four borders. The remaining pieces of fabric were enough to get creative and make
a coordinating tea towel.

I used fabric from my stash for the back of each tea towel.

half-square triangle towel

Materials

Yardages are based on 40″-wide fabrics.

If Starting with Leftovers

Assortment of yellow fabric (leftovers from *Poppies in Tuscany* and *Rays of Sunshine*)

1½″ × 8″ rectangle (leftover from *Rays of Sunshine*)

Backing: 20½″ × 20½″ square

If Starting with Yardage

Yellow: ¾ yard

Backing: ⅝ yard

Cutting

Cut 80 yellow strips 6″ long by varying widths, approximately 1½″–2¼″.

Construction

Seam allowances are ¼″ unless otherwise noted.

Half-Square Triangle Towel

MAKE THE BLOCKS

1. Sew 5 strips together to make a square that is at least 6″ × 6″. Repeat to make 16 squares and trim to 6″ × 6″. **A**

2. Cut 8 squares in half diagonally in one direction and the remaining 8 squares in the other direction. **B**

3. Mix and match the half-square triangle pieces to create 16 blocks. Sew blocks together. Press. **C**

MAKE THE TOP

1. Sew half-square triangle blocks together into 4 rows. Press.

2. Sew the rows together to complete the top. Press. **D**

MAKE THE LOOP

1. Fold the 1½″ × 8″ leftover in half right sides together to create a ¾″ × 8″ strip.

2. Sew along the length of the strip. Trim seam to ⅛″.

3. Turn right side out and press.

ASSEMBLE THE TEA TOWEL

1. Place the tea towel top right side up.

2. Put the loop along one side of the tea towel top, 2″ from the corner. Pin in place.

3. Place the 20½″ × 20½″ backing fabric right side down onto the tea towel top.

4. Sew ¼″ around the tea towel, leaving a 2″ opening along one side.

5. Trim the corners.

6. Turn right side out and press, making sure to press opening ¼″ toward the inside.

7. Close the opening using the stitch of your choice.

8. Enjoy!

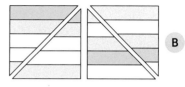

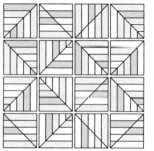

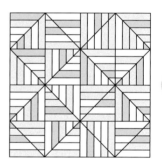

scrappy tea towel

Materials

Yardages are based on 40″-wide fabrics.

If Starting with Leftovers

3½″ × 21″ orange (leftovers from *Poppies in Tuscany* and *Rays of Sunshine*)

9¼″ × WOF light background (leftovers from *Poppies in Tuscany*)

Assorted yellow scraps (leftovers from all previous projects)

1½″ × 8″ purple sashing strip (leftover from *Rays of Sunshine)*

Backing: 20½″ × 20½″ square

If Starting with Yardage

Orange: ⅛ yard

Light: ¼ yard

Yellow: ¼ yard

Backing: ⅝ yard

Cutting

Cut 3½″ × 21″ orange leftover into 2 strips 1¾″ × 20½″.

Cut 9¼″ × WOF light leftover into 1 rectangle 4¾″ × 20½″ and 2 rectangles 4½″ × 20½″.

Cut 52 yellow squares 1⅝″ × 1⅝″.

Cut 8 yellow strips 1⅝″ × 1¾″.

Cut 8 yellow strips 1⅝″ × 2″.

Cut 2 yellow strips 1″ × 20½″.

Construction

Seam allowances are ¼″ unless otherwise noted.

Make the Strips

1. Sew together 13 yellow squares 1⅝″ × 1⅝″, 2 yellow rectangles 1⅝″ × 1¾″, and 2 yellow rectangles 1⅝″ × 2″ to create a strip 1⅝″ × 20½″. Mix and match the pieces to create variety.

2. Repeat 3 more times to create 4 strips.

Make the Top

Assemble the pieces as shown, then sew together to make the top. **E**

MAKE THE LOOP

1. Fold the 1½″ × 8″ sashing strip leftover in half right sides together to create a ¾″ × 8″ strip.

2. Sew along the length of the strip. Trim seam to ⅛″.

3. Turn right side out and press.

ASSEMBLE THE TEA TOWEL

1. Place the tea towel top right side up.

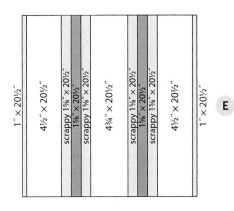

2. Put the loop along one side of the tea towel top, 2″ from the corner. Pin in place.

3. Place the 20½″ × 20½″ backing fabric right side down onto the tea towel top.

4. Sew ¼″ around the tea towel, leaving a 2″ opening along one side.

5. Trim the corners.

6. Turn right side out and press, making sure to press opening ¼″ toward the inside.

7. Close the opening using the stitch of your choice.

8. Enjoy!

Rest

FINISHED KEYBOARD WRIST REST: 3″ × 12″
FINISHED MOUSE WRIST REST: 3½″ × 5″

I COULD NOT FIGURE OUT WHAT TO DO WITH THE 3½″ × 3½″ LEFTOVER SQUARES. I tried to make a few different ideas come to life, and after some trial and error, I landed on a keyboard wrist rest and mouse pad wrist rest. These are both fairly simple to make and are so useful that my husband actually *took the wrist rest* I made! He loves it, and you will, too.

Materials

Yardages are based on 40˝-wide fabrics.

Keyboard Wrist Rest

IF STARTING WITH LEFTOVERS

8 leftover squares 3½˝ × 3½˝

Or

2 strips of fabric 3½˝ × 12½˝

IF STARTING WITH YARDAGE

⅛ yard

Additional Materials FOR BOTH LEFTOVERS AND YARDAGE

Lavender, rice, sawdust, walnut shells, or other filling of choice

Construction

Seam allowances are ¼˝ unless otherwise noted.

If you are making the wrist rest from scraps, start at Step 1. If you are making the wrist rest from strips of fabric, proceed to Step 2.

1. Sew 4 squares together to create a 3½˝ × 12½˝ strip. Repeat to make 2 strips.

2. Sew the strips right sides together, leaving one small end open.

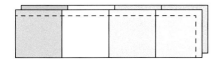

3. Fill wrist rest with filling of choice.

4. Fold the opening in ¼˝ and sew closed using your stitch of choice.

Materials

Yardages are based on 40˝-wide fabrics.

Mouse Rest

5½˝ × 7½˝ scrap

Lavender, rice, sawdust, or other filling of choice

Construction

Seam allowances are ¼˝ unless otherwise noted.

1. Fold fabric in half to measure 3¾˝ × 5½˝.

2. Sew around edges of the wrist rest, leaving a 2˝ opening along the top.

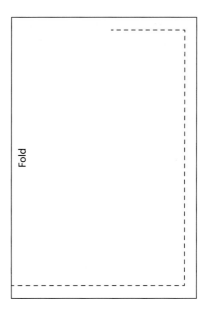

3. Fill wrist rest with filling of choice.

4. Fold the opening in ¼˝ and sew closed using your stitch of choice.

Good Hair Day

FINISHED HEADBAND: 15″ × 2¼″ (not including the elastic)

YEARS AGO, I HAD A FABRIC HEADBAND I LOVED. WHILE I WAS PIECING *POPPIES IN Tuscany*, I ran across it and decided a headband would be a perfect idea to make out of leftover fabric. I love it so much that I've made a few more. They are comfortable and easy to throw in the wash after a few wears.

Materials

Yardages are based on 40″-wide fabrics.

If Starting with Leftovers

2 rectangles 3″ × 16″

If Starting with Yardage

⅛ yard

Additional Materials
FOR BOTH LEFTOVERS AND YARDAGE

6½″ piece of ⅜″ elastic

Construction

Seam allowances are ¼″ unless otherwise noted.

1. Fold each rectangle of fabric in half, right sides together, to measure 3″ × 8″.

2. Place the Headband template (page 126) along the fold and cut 2. **A**

3. Press narrow ends in ¼″ to the wrong side of the fabric. **B**

4. Place headbands right sides facing and sew together along the long sides.

5. Turn right side out and press.

6. Place elastic ¼″ into the narrow ends of headband. Pin in place and adjust for your fit, then edgestitch around entire headband to secure, backstitching to secure the elastic. **C**

7. Enjoy!

Creating a More Sustainable Studio

The most significant way to reduce scraps is to buy only what is needed and what will be used. However, quiltmaking is nuanced and it's not always that easy; often we don't have a particular project in mind or have to guess at the yardage required.

Here are a few ideas to organize scraps so you don't throw away any fabric.

1. Host a fabric and/or craft exchange with local creatives.

2. Cut leftover fabric into rectangles, squares, or triangles and store in bins. Keep the pieces uniform (1½″ squares, 2″ squares, 3″ × 6″ rectangles, etc.)

3. Keep leftover binding to use on small or scrappy projects.

4. Make a boro quilt.

5. Use very small scraps to fill pillow forms, or use as filling in stuffed animals.

6. As a last resort, put natural materials in a compost bin.

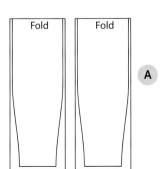

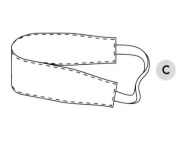

Bookmarks, Two Ways

FINISHED BOOKMARK: 2″ × 6½″

I NEVER SEEM TO HAVE ENOUGH. BOOKMARKS, TWO WAYS GIVES YOU TWO methods to make bookmarks. The tassel bookmark is traditional with tassels and I added beads from woven ribbon barrettes I've had since childhood! The elastic bookmark is a favorite because you can increase or decrease elastic length and make it fit around a variety of book sizes.

Materials

If Starting with Leftovers

TASSEL BOOKMARK

1 rectangle 4½″ × 7″ or piece scraps to make this size

ELASTIC BOOKMARK

2 rectangles 2½″ × 7″ or piece scraps to make this size

If Starting with Yardage

1 precut 10″ square

Additional Materials

FOR BOTH LEFTOVERS AND YARDAGE

1 piece of ribbon 10″ long for tassel bookmark

Optional: Beads for tassel bookmark

1 piece of ⅜″ elastic 10″ long for elastic bookmark

Construction

Seam allowances are ¼″ unless otherwise noted.

Tassel Bookmark

1. Fold the rectangle in half to 2¼″ × 7″, right sides together.

2. Fold ribbon in half and pin to the inside of the bookmark at the center of the top. **A**

3. Sew across the top and down the side, leaving bottom edge without ribbon open. **B**

4. Clip corners, then turn right side out.

5. Press, making sure to press the open edge ¼″ toward the inside of the bookmark, then edgestitch around all edges.

6. Attach beads to tassel, if desired, and enjoy!

Elastic Bookmark

1. Place 2 rectangles 2″ × 7″, right sides together.

2. Pin elastic between the two layers at each end. **C**

3. Sew around the edges, leaving a 2″ gap along one side. **D**

4. Clip corners, then turn right side out.

5. Press, making sure to press the open edge ¼″ toward the inside of the bookmark, then edgestitch around all edges.

6. Enjoy!

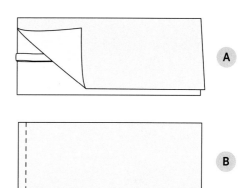

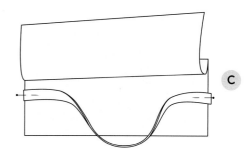

Keep It Together

FINISHED SIZE: 4¼″ × 5⅜″

AS FABRIC LEFTOVERS WHITTLED DOWN, IT BECAME INCREASINGLY TOUGH TO figure out what to make with what I had remaining. The cord keeper was no exception. Normally I'd put these pieces into a scrap bin. The idea came to me while I was looking for an extension cord in my husband's office and saw a hook and loop tie keeping cords organized. Voilà! Perfect small project to make with the little bit of leftovers I had.

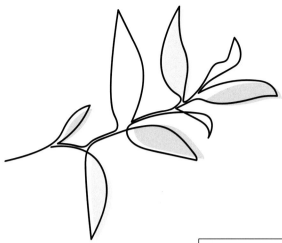

Materials

2 rectangles 4¾″ × 5⅞″ leftover or scrap

1½″ piece of hook and loop tape

Construction

Seam allowances are ¼″ unless otherwise noted.

1. Place rectangles right sides together.

2. Sew ¼″ around the edges, leaving a 2″ gap along the bottom edge. **A**

3. Clip corners, then turn right side out and press.

4. Edgestitch around all edges.

5. Sew hook side of the tape to one end of the cord keeper. Sew the loop side of the tape to the opposite end and on the other side of the cord keeper. **B**

6. Enjoy!

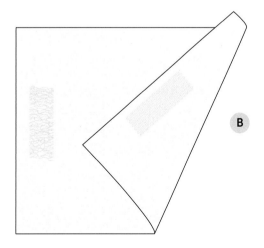

Keep in Touch

FINISHED SIZE: varies

I HAD A RANDOM ASSORTMENT OF SCRAPS THAT DIDN'T MAKE SENSE TO ME
after creating the other projects in this chapter. After much consternation, I realized that sometimes the simplest solution is also the best solution. To make sense of the bits and baubles, I
turned to two tried-and-true scrap busters: fabric tape and postcards.

Carpet tape, which is double sided, comes in many different widths. I used 1½″ carpet tape and placed scraps on one side of it any which way I wanted. It didn't need to make sense. The tape is a fun way to decorate gifts, packages, and envelopes, or use it to make a fun set of postcards as a small gift for a teacher, hostess, or friend.

Materials

Assorted scraps

1½″ carpet tape

Card stock

Construction

Fabric Tape

1. Open carpet tape and press the wrong side of fabric to the sticky side of the tape.

2. When you are ready to use the fabric tape, cut to size, remove plastic backing, and apply to packages.

TIP

I trim my scraps to the width of the carpet tape; however, you can trim scraps after securing it to the tape or you can leave it slightly wider than the tape to create a little fringe along the edge.

Postcards

1. Cut card stock into 3½″ × 5″ rectangles.

2. Cut 3 pieces of carpet tape 5″ each.

3. Press carpet tape to one side of the card stock, removing plastic backing as you go. Overlap each piece slightly and trim as needed.

4. Collage scraps to the postcards.

5. Enjoy!

Misunderstood

FINISHED BLOCKS: 3˝ × 6˝ and 1½˝ × 3˝ • FINISHED QUILT: 66½˝ × 75½˝

I STARTED THIS QUILT KNOWING THE COLORS I WANTED TO USE AND THAT I wanted a quilt with movement, but I didn't have a finished quilt designed. Ultimately, the process was an exercise in creativity, play, and how to manipulate value and hue for maximum impact on a final design. *Misunderstood* is made entirely from Flying Geese blocks and the combination of a versatile block with a variety of fabrics and color created the movement.

Misunderstood was pieced primarily with scraps and small amounts of yardage where I needed to fill in some gaps. I even had the backing and binding fabric sitting on my shelf waiting for this quilt! As I noted in How to Use Your Stash Efficiently (page 15), you do not need all your fabrics to match exactly. Gather fabrics that play nicely together in a group. Once you have your fabrics selected, put them into five broad categories from lightest to darkest. My color scheme is white, sky blue, medium blue, dark blue, and navy.

Materials

Yardages are based on 40˝- wide fabrics.

Lightest: 1⅞ yards

Light: 1¾ yards

Medium: 2⅜ yards

Dark: 2⅜ yards

Darkest: 1½ yards

Backing: 4⅔ yards

Binding: ⅝ yard for bias binding

Batting: 75˝ × 84˝

Starch or a starch alternative

Cutting

Refer to Basic Block Construction (page 16) for half-square triangle and quarter-square triangle instructions.

TIP

Because of all the bias in this quilt, I *highly* recommend you use starch or a starch alternative on your fabrics before you cut. This, and pressing gently, will help keep your blocks and the finished quilt from becoming distorted.

Lightest

Cut 11 squares 7½˝ × 7½˝. Subcut into quarter-square triangles.

Cut 12 squares 4½˝ × 4½˝. Subcut into quarter-square triangles.

Cut 31 squares 4˝ × 4˝. Subcut into half-square triangles.

Cut 54 squares 2½˝ × 2½˝. Subcut into half-square triangles.

Light

Cut 7 squares 7½˝ × 7½˝. Subcut into quarter-square triangles.

Cut 10 squares 4½˝ × 4½˝. Subcut into quarter-square triangles.

Cut 40 squares 4˝ × 4˝. Subcut into half-square triangles.

Cut 61 squares 2½˝ × 2½˝. Subcut into half-square triangles.

Medium

Cut 13 squares 7½˝ × 7½˝. Subcut into quarter-square triangles.

Cut 21 squares 4½˝ × 4½˝. Subcut into quarter-square triangles.

Cut 46 squares 4˝ × 4˝. Subcut into half-square triangles.

Cut 86 squares 2½˝ × 2½˝. Subcut into half-square triangles.

Dark

Cut 13 squares 7½˝ × 7½˝. Subcut into quarter-square triangles.

Cut 19 squares 4½˝ × 4½˝. Subcut into quarter-square triangles.

Cut 63 squares 4˝ × 4˝. Subcut into half-square triangles.

Cut 64 squares 2½˝ × 2½˝. Subcut into half-square triangles.

Darkest

Cut 8 squares 7½˝ × 7½˝. Subcut into quarter-square triangles.

Cut 14 squares 4½˝ × 4½˝. Subcut into quarter-square triangles.

Cut 21 squares 4˝ × 4˝. Subcut into half-square triangles.

Cut 36 squares 2½˝ × 2½˝. Subcut into half-square triangles.

Construction

Seam allowances are ¼″ unless otherwise noted.

Block Assembly

You will make 200 Flying Geese 3″ × 6″ and 298 Flying Geese 1½″ × 3″. I chose to make traditional Flying Geese so I could achieve the color flow and movement I desired.

TIP

The half-square and quarter-square triangles from the 2½″ and 4½″ squares make 1½″ × 3″ Flying Geese and the half-square and quarter-square triangles from the 4″ and 7½″ squares make 3″ × 6″ Flying Geese.

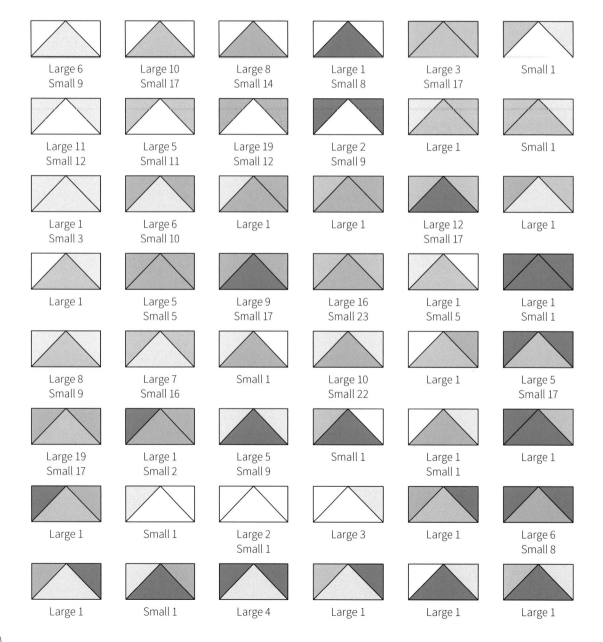

Large 6 / Small 9   Large 10 / Small 17   Large 8 / Small 14   Large 1 / Small 8   Large 3 / Small 17   Small 1

Large 11 / Small 12   Large 5 / Small 11   Large 19 / Small 12   Large 2 / Small 9   Large 1   Small 1

Large 1 / Small 3   Large 6 / Small 10   Large 1   Large 1   Large 12 / Small 17   Large 1

Large 1   Large 5 / Small 5   Large 9 / Small 17   Large 16 / Small 23   Large 1 / Small 5   Large 1 / Small 1

Large 8 / Small 9   Large 7 / Small 16   Small 1   Large 10 / Small 22   Large 1   Large 5 / Small 17

Large 19 / Small 17   Large 1 / Small 2   Large 5 / Small 9   Small 1   Large 1 / Small 1   Large 1

Large 1   Small 1   Large 2 / Small 1   Large 3   Large 1   Large 6 / Small 8

Large 1   Small 1   Large 4   Large 1   Large 1   Large 1

TRADITIONAL FLYING GEESE

1. With right sides together, sew 1 half-square triangle to 1 quarter-square triangle. The triangles will line up along the bottom and the bunny ear will extend ¼″ along the top. Press toward the small triangle. **A–B**

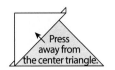

2. Repeat along the opposite side using another half-square triangle. Press toward the small triangle. **C–D**

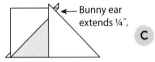

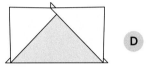

3. Align the 45° angle of the ruler along the seamline of the Flying Geese block. Leave a ¼″ seam allowance at the top. Trim the top of the block. **E**

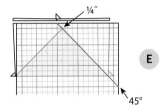

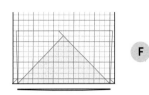

4. Place the ruler along the bottom of the Flying Geese block and trim between the points. **F**

5. Find the center point of the unfinished width of the block (1¾″ for the small Flying Geese and 3¼″ for the large Flying Geese). Align the 45° angle of the ruler along the seam line of the Flying Geese and the center measurement. Trim the right side. **G**

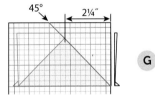

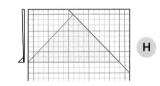

6. Repeat on the left side. **H**

Quilt Construction

1. Sew the quilt together in sections as shown below. All blocks are sewn right sides together.

2. Some sections have partial seams. To make a partial seam, place a smaller block on top of a larger block, right sides together. Sew from the middle of the block to the outer edge, making sure to backstitch to lock the seam in place. Press toward the small block. **A–B**

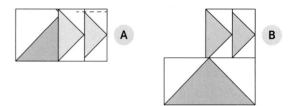

QUILT ASSEMBLY

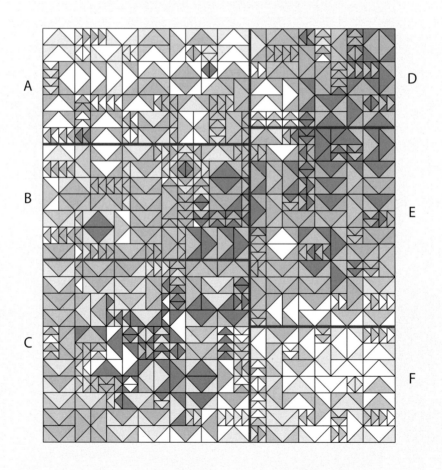

3. Sew the entire length of another block to the completed section. Press toward the outer block. Repeat. **C–E**

4. Sew the last block to the section. **F**

5. Fold the assembly and sew the partial seam closed. **G–H**

Finishing

Quilt, bind, and enjoy!

In the know. Conventional cotton is the third largest user of pesticides in the United States. The World Health Organization labeled the popular pesticide, glysophate, as a probable carcinogen in 2019.[10]

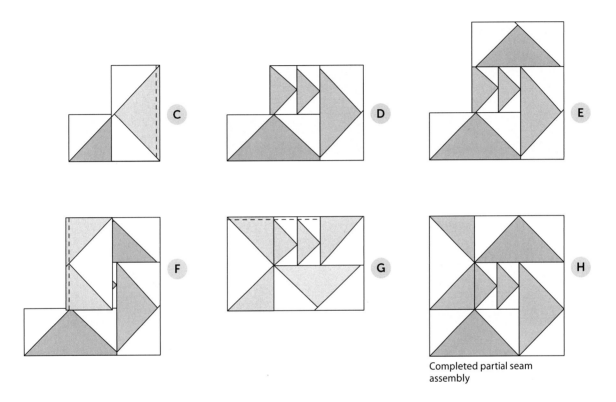

Completed partial seam assembly

Cutting the Leftovers

Unlike the previous project groups, I approached the leftovers from *Misunderstood* differently. Instead of cutting the leftovers by project, I cut them all down before I started anything new. This challenged me to explore options using half- and quarter-square triangles. It was a different approach that invited me to play with the concept: What happens when you have leftovers cut into a specific shape, or shapes, without a plan?

After creating *Misunderstood* you will have an assortment of pieces *and* some yardage left over. Directions on the next page show you how to cut remaining yardage to make piano keys and how to cut any leftover square or rectangle pieces to make quarter- and half-square triangles.

---

10. Jessica Shade, PhD, Kathleen Delate, PhD. (2020) Organic Cotton: One of the Most Important Choices You Can Make for the Environment The Organic Center.

Cut the Following from the Remaining Yardage

Lightest

Cut 1 strip 2″ × WOF.

Cut 2 strips 1½″ × WOF.

Light

Cut 3 strips 1½″ × WOF.

Medium

Cut 1 strip 2″ × WOF.

Cut 2 strips 1¾″ × WOF.

Cut 2 strips 1¼″ × 11″*.

Cut 2 strips 1¼″ × 9½″*.

* These strips will become the inner borders for the *Tea at Twilight* tea mat (page 115). I had enough medium blue to cut these, but you may have extra in another color. Whatever fabric you can cut this from is what you should use.

Dark

Cut 4 strips 1¾″ × WOF.

Darkest

Cut 4 strips 1½″ × WOF.

Cut the Following from a Wide Variety of the Leftover Scraps

Refer to Basic Block Construction (page 16) for half-square triangle and quarter-square triangle instructions.

Cut 14 squares 7½″ × 7½″. Subcut into 56 quarter-squares 3¾″ × 3¾″, and then subcut into 112 half-square triangles.

Cut 21 squares 4½″ × 4½″. Subcut into half-square triangles.

Cut 45 squares 4″ × 4″. Subcut into half-square triangles.

Cut 60 squares 2½″ × 2½″. Subcut into half-square triangles.

Construction

Seam allowances are ¼″ unless otherwise noted.

Mix and match fabric to make the following half- and quarter-square triangle blocks from *Misunderstood* leftovers.

1. Make 60 half-square triangles 2″ × 2″ unfinished.

2. Make 45 half-square triangles 3½″ × 3½″ unfinished.

3. Make 28 half-square triangles 4″ × 4″ unfinished.

4. Make 30 quarter-square triangle blocks 4½″ × 4½″ unfinished, using the remaining quarter-square and half-square triangle pieces.

TIP

I combined half-square triangles and quarter-square triangles that were the same size and when I ran out, I mixed and matched. For example, I used a 4″ half-square triangle unit and a 4½″ half-square triangle unit to create a 4″ half-square triangle. There is minimal waste but I don't have a rogue triangle of fabric remaining.

Make Piano Keys

1. Sew the WOF strips together randomly to make an approximately 20″ × WOF piece.

2. Subcut into 8 sections 5″ × approximately 20″.

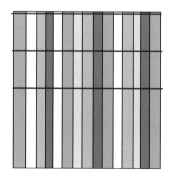

Misunderstood Medallion

FINISHED QUILT: 50½″ × 50½″

I'VE WANTED TO MAKE A MEDALLION QUILT FOR A LONG TIME AND THE leftover pieces screamed at me to use them for just that. Half- and quarter-square triangle blocks and piano keys are set off in a deep blue batik to create a dramatic statement. This quilt is simple but packs a punch and was the perfect way to use remaining fabric.

The background and backing fabrics were pulled from my stash to round out the project.

I actually mis-cut the background fabric while making this quilt (bad math) and pulled a second fabric from my stash to use with the half made quilt for my background.

Materials

Yardages are based on 40″-wide fabrics.

If Starting with Leftovers

36 half-square triangles 3½″ × 3½″

28 quarter-square triangles 4½″ × 4½″

60 half-square triangles 2″ × 2″

5 piano key sections

If Starting with Yardage

Light to Medium: 1⅜ yards

Medium to Dark: 1⅜ yards

Additional Materials

FOR BOTH LEFTOVERS AND YARDAGE

Background Fabric*: 1½ yards

Backing: 3⅓ yards

Binding: ⅝ yard for bias binding

Batting: 59″ × 59″

*If you are using a batik or other fabric that is at least 43″ wide, you can get away with 1⅓ yards.

Cutting

Refer to Basic Block Construction (page 16) for half-square triangle and quarter-square triangle instructions.

If Starting with Yardage

LIGHT TO MEDIUM

Cut 2 strips 6″ × WOF. Subcut into 7 squares 6″ × 6″. Subcut into quarter-square triangles.

Cut 3 strips 4½″ × WOF. Subcut into 18 squares 4½″ × 4½″. Subcut into half-square triangles.

Cut 2 strips 2½″ × WOF. Subcut into 30 squares 2½″ × 2½″. Subcut into half-square triangles.

Cut 5 strips 1½″ × WOF.

MEDIUM TO DARK

Cut 2 strips 6″ × WOF. Subcut into 7 squares 6″ × 6″. Subcut into quarter-square triangles.

Cut 3 strips 4½″ × WOF. Subcut into 18 squares 4½″ × 4½″. Subcut into half-square triangles.

Cut 2 strips 2½″ × WOF. Subcut into 30 squares 2½″ × 2½″. Subcut into half-square triangles.

Cut 5 strips 1½″ × WOF.

Background

Cut 10 strips 3½″ × WOF.

Subcut 3 strips into:

  2 rectangles 3½″ × 18½″

  2 rectangles 3½″ × 24½″

Subcut 2 strips into:

  2 rectangles 3½″ × 19″

  2 rectangles 3½″ × 20½″

Set aside the last 5 strips for the final border.

Cut 3 strips 2″ × WOF. Subcut into 2 rectangles 2″ × 20″ and 2 rectangles 2″ × 23″.

Cut 4 strips 1½″ × WOF. Subcut into:

  2 rectangles 1½″ × 32½″

  2 rectangles 1½″ × 34½″

Construction

Seam allowances are ¼˝ unless otherwise noted.

Refer to Basic Block Construction (page 16) for half-square triangle and quarter-square triangle instructions.

Make Half-Square Triangles

1. Mix and match the 4½˝ half-square triangle pieces to make 36 half-square triangle units. Trim to 3½˝ × 3½˝.

2. Mix and match the 2½˝ half-square triangle pieces to make 60 half-square triangle units. Trim to 2˝ × 2˝.

Make Quarter-Square Triangles

Mix and match the 6˝ quarter-square triangles to make 28 quarter-square triangle units. Trim to 4½˝ × 4½˝.

Make the Piano Keys

1. Sew 10 strips 1½˝ × WOF together. Press.

2. Cut 16 strips 2½˝ × 10½˝ wide.

3. Sew 4 sets of strips together to make a 2½˝ × 40½˝ strip.

4. Repeat Step 3 so you have 4 piano keys strip sets.

If starting with the previously made piano keys, cut 5 piano key strips 5˝ × 20˝ in half to make 2½˝ × 20˝ strips. Sew these together end to end and cut into 4 strips 2½˝ × ½˝. If necessary add more 2½˝ strips to the piano keys.

Assemble the Quilt

1. Sew 36 half-square triangles 3½˝ × 3½˝ together to create the center medallion. **A**

2. Sew a 3½˝ × 18½˝ background rectangle to the top and bottom of the medallion. Press.

3. Sew a 3½˝ × 24½˝ background rectangle to the remaining two sides of the medallion. Press. **B**

4. Sew 2 sets of 6 quarter-square triangle units 4½˝ × 4½˝ together. Press.

5. Sew to opposite sides of the medallion.

6. Sew 2 sets of 8 quarter-square triangle units together. Press.

7. Sew to remaining two sides of the medallion. **C**

8. For the remaining borders, refer to the assembly diagram (page 110). Sew a 1½˝ × 32½˝ rectangle to the top and bottom of the medallion. Press.

9. Sew a 1½˝ × 34½˝ rectangle to the remaining two sides of the medallion. Press.

10. Sew the 2½˝ × 40½˝ piano key borders to the quilt, following directions in How to Miter Corners (page 18).

11. Sew 13 of the 2˝ × 2˝ half-square triangles together, noting the diagonal direction, and press. Repeat to make 2.

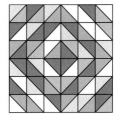
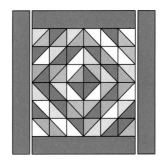

12. Sew a 2″ × 20″ rectangle next to the strips from Step 11. Press.

13. Sew a 3½″ × 19″ rectangle to the end of the strips from Step 12. Press **D**

14. Sew the border units to opposite sides of the quilt, making sure the half-square triangles are on the outside.

15. Sew a 2″ × 2″ half-square triangle to a 2″ × 23″ rectangle and press. Repeat to make 2.

16. Sew 16 of the remaining 2″ × 2″ half square triangles together, then press. Repeat to make 2.

17. Sew the strip of half-square triangles from Step 16 to the half-square triangle/inner border unit. Make 2.

18. Sew a 3½″ × 20½″ rectangle to the end of each unit from Step 17 and press. **E**

19. Sew these borders to the top and bottom of the quilt.

20. Trim off the selvages and sew the 5 remaining 3½″ × WOF background strips together.

21. Subcut 2 strips 3½″ × 44½″. Sew to the sides of the quilt. Press.

22. Subcut 2 strips 3½″ × 50½″. Sew to the top and bottom of the quilt. Press.

Finishing

Quilt, bind, and enjoy!

QUILT ASSEMBLY

Feeling Blue Tote Bag

FINISHED BAG: 11½″ wide × 12″ tall × 6½″ deep

THIS PROJECT HAD SEVERAL POSSIBLE ITERATIONS, BUT I LANDED ON A TOTE
bag. While I'm not usually one for quilted tote bags, I must somewhat hesitantly share that I absolutely adore this one! And the bow takes it to another level altogether. This project comes together really quickly, and I was happy to pull the lining fabric from my stash.

Materials

Yardages are based on 40˝-wide fabrics.

If Starting with Leftovers

25 half-square triangles 4˝ × 4˝

2 piano key sections

Leftover dark fabric from *Misunderstood*

Leftover background fabric from *Misunderstood Medallion*

If Starting with Yardage

Light to medium fabric: ⅝ yard assorted scraps

Medium to dark fabric: ¾ yard assorted scraps

Additional Materials

FOR BOTH LEFTOVERS AND YARDAGE

Lining and handles: ¾ yard

Fusible interfacing: 2 yards of 20˝ wide

Cardboard: 6˝ × 11˝ rectangle

Cutting

Refer to Basic Block Construction (page 16) for half-square triangle cutting instructions.

If Starting with Yardage

LIGHT TO MEDIUM

Cut 2 strips 5˝ × WOF. Subcut into 13 squares 5˝ × 5˝; subcut into half-square triangles.

Cut 3 strips 1½˝ × WOF.

MEDIUM TO DARK

Cut 2 strips 5˝ × WOF. Subcut into 12 squares 5˝ × 5˝; subcut into half-square triangles.

Cut 2 rectangles 4˝ × 4½˝.

Cut 1 strip 3½˝ × WOF; subcut into 1 rectangle 3½˝ × 36˝ for bow.

Cut 1 strip 2˝ × WOF; subcut 2 strips 2˝ × 18˝.

Cut 3 strips 1½˝ × WOF.

Interfacing

Cut 2 rectangles 4˝ × 19½˝.

Cut 2 rectangles 18˝ × 30˝.

Lining

Cut 1 rectangle 18˝ × 30˝.

Cut 2 rectangles 4½˝ × 20.

Construction

Seam allowances are ¼˝ unless otherwise noted.

Make the Half-Square Triangles

Refer to Basic Block Construction (page 16) for half-square triangle instructions.

Make 25 half-square triangle units from the 5˝ squares. Trim to 4˝ × 4˝.

Make the Piano Keys

If using leftovers, trim 2 sections to 5˝ × 18˝.

IF USING YARDAGE:

1. Trim off the selvage edges and sew the 1½˝ × WOF strips together.

2. Crosscut into 8 sections 5˝ × 6½˝.

3. Sew 3 sections together and trim to 5˝ × 18˝. Repeat to make 2.

Make the Outside of the Tote

1. Arrange the 25 half-square triangles in 5 rows of 5.

2. Sew together into rows and then sew the rows together.

3. Sew a 2″ × 18″ dark rectangle to opposite sides of the square. Press.

4. Sew a 5″ × 18″ piano key rectangle to the tote bag. Press. **A**

4. Press an 18″ × 30″ rectangle of interfacing to the wrong side of the lining fabric and the wrong side of the tote bag cover.

Make the Handles

1. Press the interfacing to the wrong side of the 4½″ × 20″ rectangles. The interfacing is slightly smaller to reduce bulk.

2. Sew the rectangle in half lengthwise, right sides together.

3. Turn right side out and press. Sew ⅛ inch away from each edge. **B**

Make the Pockets

1. From the leftover lining, cut 2 rectangles 4″ × 4½″.

2. Pair each rectangle with a 4″ × 4½″ rectangle leftover background fabric to create a pocket.

3. Sew together, leaving a 2″ opening on one side for turning.

TIP
I used two pieces of leftover lining fabric and two pieces of leftover background fabric so I would have two fully faced pockets.

4. Turn the pockets right side out and press. Close the seam by hand using a slip stitch, or with a straight stitch on your machine.

5. Pin the pockets to each side of the lining fabric in desired location. Edgestitch around 3 sides of the pocket, making sure to leave the top of the pocket open.

Make the Bow

1. Fold a 3½″ × 36″ leftover rectangle of background fabric in half lengthwise and press.

2. At each end, mark 3″ from the end along the fold. Sew a diagonal line between the mark and the corner of the fabric. Trim.

3. Sew along the long edge of the rectangle, leaving a 2″ opening in the center.

4. Turn bow right side out. Use a point turner to the ends of the bow. Press.

5. Stitch opening closed by machine or hand.

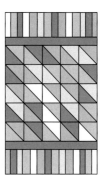
A

B

Assembling the Bag

1. Pin the handles 6″ from each outside edge of the front of the tote bag.

2. Pin or thread baste into place. **C**

3. Fold the cover of the bag in half, wrong sides together, to find the center. Repeat for the lining fabric.

4. Cut a 3″ × 3″ square on the bottom right and bottom left of the tote bag and the lining. **D**

5. Sew the sides of the bag together. Backstitch when you start and stop to lock the seam into place.

6. Sew the sides of the lining together. Leave a 4″ opening along one side. Backstitch where you start and stop to lock the seam into place.

7. With right sides together, match the bottom center fold of the bag with the side seam. Secure with a pin and sew together to create the base of the bag. Backstitch when you start and stop to lock the seam into place. Repeat this step with the lining fabric. **E**

8. Matching the right side of the bag to the right side of the lining, place bag cover into the lining.

9. Sew around the top of the bag.

10. Turn the bag right side out through the opening in the lining and press. Stitch the opening closed.

11. Edgestitch the top of the bag. **F**

12. Wrap bow around one of the handles.

Make the Base

1. Use 2 leftover background rectangles 3½″ × 15½″ to create the bottom of the base. Sew together to make a 6½″ × 15½″ piece. Trim to 6½″ × 12″.

2. Sew any remaining scraps together to make a 6½″ × 12″ rectangle for the top of the base.

3. Sew the two rectangles together to make a 12½″ × 12″ rectangle.

4. Fold down ¼″ along one 12½″ edge. Press and then fold down ⅜″. Press and edgestitch the hem.

5. Fold the base in half, right sides together, and sew the bottom and side together.

6. Slide the pocket over the cardboard.

7. Place into bottom of the bag and enjoy!

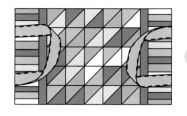

C

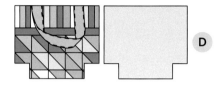

D

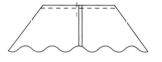

E

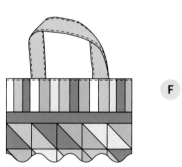

F

Tea at Twilight

FINISHED MAT: 14″ × 14″

I LIKE TO ENJOY A CUP OF TEA AND A SNACK WHEN I SEW. FOR YEARS I'VE PUT A plate and mug across the room on my desk to keep crumbs and accidental spills away from my current project; however, I always grumble when I have to actually get up for them. When I was looking at the leftover pieces I had from projects in this chapter, I decided that they'd make a perfect tea mat—enough to make something small, adorable, and useful. Favorite color, favorite block, favorite snack, and beverage closer to me. A win all around!

Materials

Yardages are based on 40″-wide fabrics.

If Starting with Leftovers

9 half-square triangles 3½″ × 3½″

2 rectangles 1¼″ × 9½″ leftover from *Misunderstood*

2 rectangles 1¼″ × 11″ leftover from *Misunderstood*

2 rectangles 2″ × 11″ leftover from *Misunderstood*

2 rectangles 2″ × 14″ leftover from *Misunderstood*

1 rectangle 4½″ × 22″ leftover from *Feeling Blue Tote Bag*

1 rectangle 3½″ × 16″ leftover from *Feeling Blue Tote Bag*

Backing: leftover 10″ × 18″ lining from *Feeling Blue Tote Bag*

Binding: leftover piano keys

If Starting with Yardage

Yardages are based on 40″-wide fabrics.

Light: ⅛ yard

Dark: ⅛ yard

Inner Border: ⅛ yard

Outer Border: ⅛ yard

Backing: ½ yard

Binding: ⅛ yard

Additional Materials

FOR BOTH LEFTOVERS AND YARDAGE

Batting: 16″ × 16″

Cutting

If Starting with Leftovers

Trim the 4½″ × 22″ rectangle to 4½″ × 16″. Trim the 10″ × 18″ leftover lining piece to 10″ × 16″.

Cut the piano keys into 4 rectangles 2″ × 14½″.

If Starting with Yardage

LIGHT

Cut 1 strip 4″ × WOF. Subcut 5 squares 4″ × 4″. Cut into half-square triangles.

DARK

Cut 1 strip 4″ × WOF. Subcut 5 squares 4″ × 4″. Cut into half-square triangles

INNER BORDER

Cut 1 strip 1¼″ × WOF. Subcut 2 strips 1¼″ × 9½″ and 2 strips 1¼″ × 11″.

OUTER BORDER

Cut 2 strips 2″ × WOF. Subcut 2 strips 2″ × 11″ and 2 strips 2″ × 14″.

Backing

Cut 1 square 16″ × 16″.

Binding

Cut 2 strips 2″ × WOF.

Construction

Seam allowances are ¼″ unless otherwise noted.

Make the Half-Square Triangles

Refer to Basic Block Construction (page 16) for half-square triangle instructions.

Make 9 half-square triangle units from the 4″ squares. Trim to 3½″ × 3½″.

Make the Tea Mat

1. Sew the 3½″ × 3½″ half-square triangles together into a 3 × 3 grid. Press. **A**

2. Sew a 1¼″ × 9½″ rectangle to opposite sides of the center square. Press.

3. Sew a 1¼″ × 11″ rectangle to the remaining sides. Press. **B**

4. Sew a 2″ × 11″ rectangle to opposite sides of the center square. Press.

5. Sew a 2″ × 14″ rectangle to the remaining two sides. Press. **C**

Make the Quilt Back

The leftover fabric for the back isn't quite large enough, so we'll sew smaller leftover blocks and pieces together to make up the difference.

1. Sew the 3½″ × 16″ rectangles to one side of the 10″ × 16″ rectangle. Press.

2. Sew the 4½″ × 16″ rectangle to the other side. Press.

Finishing

1. Quilt as desired, then trim the edges.

2. Cut the remaining 5″ × 20″ piano keys into 2 rectangles 2″ × 20″ and trim the leftover 2½″ × 20″ piano key to 2″ × 20″.

3. Sew the 3 rectangles together. Press.

4. Cut into 4 rectangles 2″ × 15″.

5. Press the piano key rectangles in half lengthwise.

6. Sew 2 sections to opposite sides of the tea mat. Press to the back and secure the binding to the tea mat by hand or machine, trimming or folding the ends as needed. **D**

7. Fold the short edges of the remaining binding ½″ toward the wrong sides. Press.

8. Sew the binding to the remaining sides. Press to the back of the mat and secure the binding to the tea mat by hand or machine. **E**

9. Enjoy!

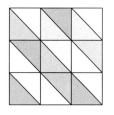

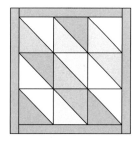

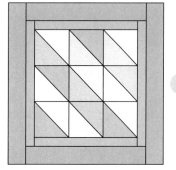

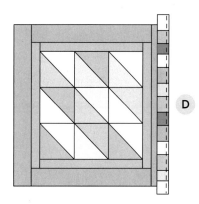

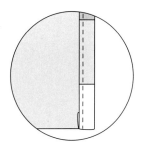

Needles on the Go Case

FINISHED CASE: 3¾″ × 7¼″

I HAD AN ODD ASSORTMENT OF SCRAP SIZES REMAINING BY THE TIME I MADE this needle case and it took me some time to figure out how to make a cohesive project with fabric that didn't necessarily fit together nicely. Enter the needle case. The perfect way to put odds and ends together in one project that makes sense! Furthermore, I'm slowly recognizing the need to keep one with each project (or WIP) so the correct needles stay easily accessible and off the floor.

Materials

Yardages are based on 40˝-wide fabrics.

If Starting with Leftovers

3 leftover 4˝ half-square triangles

Assorted leftover materials from *Feeling Blue Tote Bag* (lining, background, piano keys, etc.)

If Starting with Yardage

¼ yard assorted blue and white fabric

Additional Materials

FOR BOTH LEFTOVERS AND YARDAGE

Ribbon: 8˝

Batting: 1 rectangle 4˝ × 7½˝ and 1 rectangle 2½˝ × 3½˝

Felt: 3½˝ × 6½˝

Cutting

If Starting with Leftovers

From the tote bag lining fabric: Cut a 4˝ square.

From the background fabric from *Misunderstood Medallion*: Cut a 3½˝ × 7½˝ rectangle and a 2½˝ × 3½˝ rectangle.

From the piano keys: Cut a 2½˝ × 3½˝ rectangle.

If Starting with Yardage

Cut 3 squares 5˝ × 5˝ each. Subcut into half-square triangles.

From Any Scraps

Cut 1 rectangle 3½˝ × 7½˝.
Cut 2 rectangles 2½˝ × 3½˝.
Cut 1 square 4˝ × 4˝

Construction

Seam allowances are ¼˝ unless otherwise noted.

Refer to Basic Block Construction (page 16) for half-square triangle block instructions.

Make 4 half-square triangle blocks.

Make the Cover

1. Make the outside cover by sewing 2 half-square triangles, 4˝ × 4˝ each, together.

2. Sew 1 half-square triangle to a 4˝ × 4˝ square to make the inside of the cover. **A**

3. Make a sandwich by placing a piece of batting between the inside and outside cover pieces. The right sides of the fabric will face out. **B**

4. Cut the ribbon into 2 sections 4˝ each.

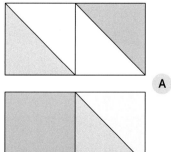

A

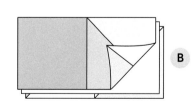

B

5. Place the ribbon in the center of short side of the cover, between the batting and the outside piece.

6. Use a straight stitch to sew ⅜″ around the edge to secure all the pieces.

7. Being careful not to cut the ribbon, use pinking shears to trim the edges of the sandwich. **C**

Make the Inside Pieces

1. Put the 3½″ × 7½″ rectangle of fabric* and the 3½″ × 7½″ rectangle of felt wrong sides together.

2. Sew ⅜″ around the edge to secure the pieces together.

3. Use pinking shears to trim the edge of the fabric.

*I had a 2½″ × 4″ scrap of fabric I sewed onto one side of the fabric. It was great way to add some dimension to the needle case and use up my leftovers. If you have other scraps, piano key leftovers or any other pieces, layering fabric inside the needle case is fun!

4. Make a sandwich by placing the 2½″ × 3½″ rectangle of batting between two 2½″ × 3½″ rectangles. The right sides of the fabric will face out.

5. Use a straight stitch to sew ⅜″ around the edge to secure all the pieces.

6. Use pinking shears to trim the edge of the fabric.

Assembly

1. Stack the cover and the inside pieces, largest to smallest. **D**

2. Measure and mark the center line.

3. Use a straight stitch to sew along the line so that all layers are secure. Backstitch to lock your seam in place.

4. Fold needle case in half and tie the ribbons in a knot or loose bow.

5. Enjoy!

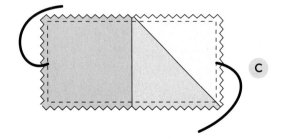

C

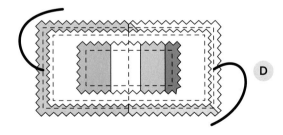

D

Sachets, Hand Warmers, Pincushions! Oh, My!

FINISHED SIZE: varies, depending on leftover block size*

OVER THE YEARS I'VE HAD FRIENDS SHARE HOW THEY LOVE LAVENDER SACHETS
and rice-filled hand warmers. They are simple to make and small leftover blocks can easily be
filled with lavender, rice, walnut shells, sawdust, or another filling of choice to make perfect hostess or teacher gifts.

---

*I was able to create one sachet with the 4½˝ × 4½˝ quarter-square triangle pieces I had remaining and one sachet with one
half-square triangle and assorted scraps. The instructions here are for a quarter-square triangle, but you can make these
any size you like.*

Materials

Yardages are based on 40˝-wide fabrics.

If Starting with Leftovers

2 half-square or quarter-square triangles 4½˝ × 4½˝

If Starting with Yardage

Assorted blue and white fabrics: ¼ yard

Additional Materials
FOR BOTH LEFTOVERS AND YARDAGE

Optional: Narrow ribbon or other trim: 5˝

Filling of choice

Cutting

If Starting with Yardage

Cut 2 squares 6˝ × 6˝. Subcut into quarter-square triangles.

If you are using ribbon, cut ribbon into 2 strips 2½˝ long.

Construction

Seam allowances are ¼˝ unless otherwise noted.

Refer to Basic Block Construction (page 16) for half-square triangle and quarter-square triangle instructions.

Make the Quarter-Square Triangles

1. Make 2 quarter-square triangle units.

2. Trim to 4½˝ × 4½˝.

Make the Sachets

1. If you are using ribbon or trim, fold it in half and place ⅜˝ from one corner on the right side of one half-square triangle block. If you are not using ribbon or trim, start at Step 2. **A**

2. Place two blocks, right sides together. Sew around the sides. Leave a space so you can turn the sachet/hand warmer/pincushion right side out. Backstitch when you start and stop to lock the seam. **B**

3. Trim corners. For this project, I trimmed at an angle along the corners. The sachet/hand warmer/pincushion is small, so trimming a little extra fabric along the sides will help reduce extra bulk going into the corner. **C**

4. Turn right side out. Press.

5. Fill with material of choice. If you are filling this with emery, make a muslin to go inside the sachet to keep the small particles in the pincushion.

6. Close opening with a needle and thread using a slip stitch.

7. Enjoy!

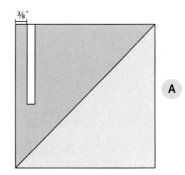

A

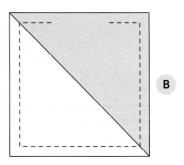

B

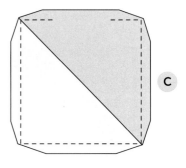

C

❝ Sustainablity is no longer about doing less harm. It's about doing more good." **JOCHEN ZEITZ**

templates

Accessing Patterns

To access the pattern through the tiny url, type the web address provided into your browser window.

tinyurl.com/11577-patterns-download

Using Patterns

Print directly from the browser window or download the pattern.

Review the complete instructions for printing and tiling included in the pattern download PDF.

• To print at home, print the letter-size pages, selecting 100% size on the printer. Use dashed/dotted lines to trim, layer, and tape together pages as needed.

• To print at a copyshop, save the full-size pages to a thumb drive or email them to your local copyshop for printing.

Poppies in Tuscany

Diamond

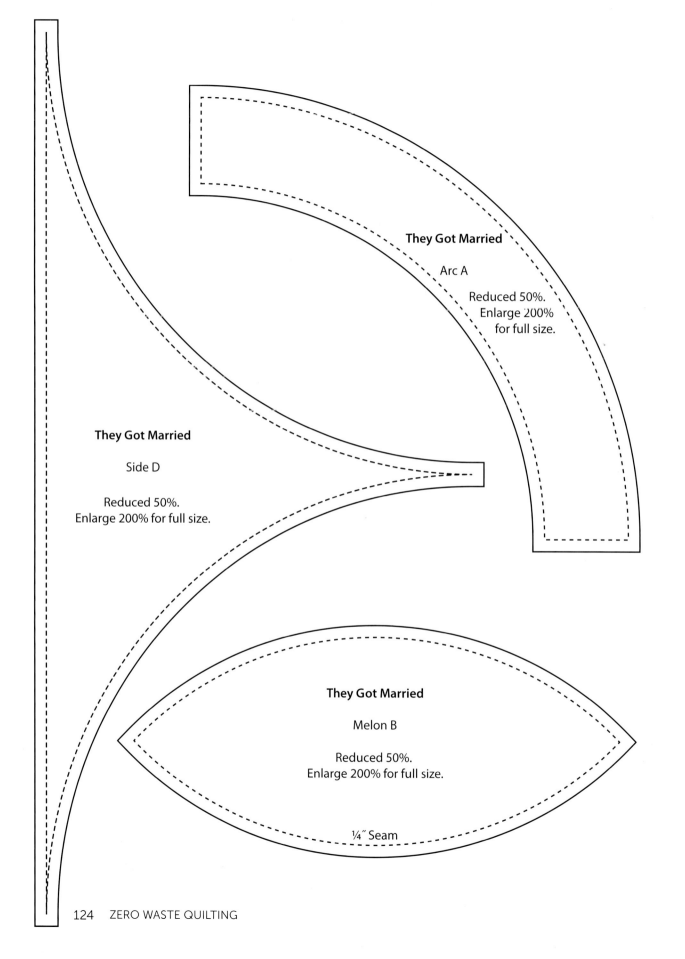

They Got Married

Arc A

Reduced 50%.
Enlarge 200%
for full size.

They Got Married

Side D

Reduced 50%.
Enlarge 200% for full size.

They Got Married

Melon B

Reduced 50%.
Enlarge 200% for full size.

¼″ Seam

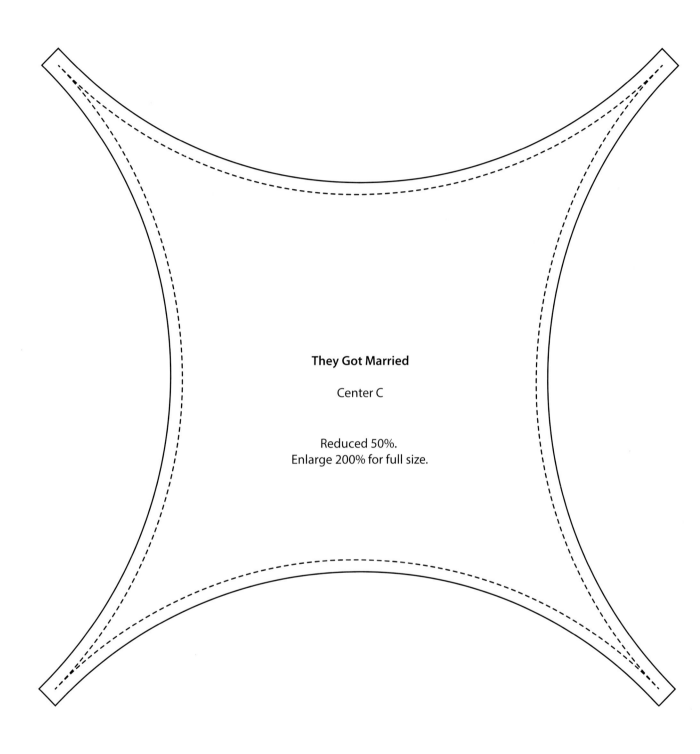

They Got Married

Center C

Reduced 50%.
Enlarge 200% for full size.

Petal Pusher Pillow

Circle

Fold

Good Hair Day Headband

Cut 2.

resources

"It really boils down to this; that all life is interrelated. We are all caught in an inescapable network of mutuality, tied in a single garment of destiny. To whatever affects one directly, affects all indirectly." **DR. MARTIN LUTHER KING, JR.**

Shop Profiles

Estate sales, yard sales, and crafty reuse stores are an excellent way to look for secondhand fabric, but when these don't pan out, there are a myriad of shops that sell scraps, deadstock fabric, natural dyes, sustainably sourced materials, and more. This is a small list to get you started.

- A Thrifty Notion is an online source for sustainable, vintage, and deadstock fabric. **athriftynotion.com**

- Audrey Louise Reynolds is an online source for handmade, natural dyes. **alrdyeing.com**

- FABSCRAP is an online fabric and notions shop with brick-and-mortar locations in New York City and Philadelphia. They pick up and resell leftovers from the garment industry. **fabscrap.org**

- FeelGood Fibers is an online shop for destashing quilting fabric. You can list destash fabric here and make a little money for when you really need to purchase a yard or two and you can feel good about the yardage you buy here knowing it came from another quilter's stash. **feelgoodfibers.com**

- Goodwill is a secondhand store that offers gently and sometimes never-used fabric, pillow inserts, and other craft items donated by individuals. **goodwill.org**

- Queen of Raw is an online site dedicated to reselling sustainable and deadstock fabrics, keeping them out of landfills. **resale.queenofraw.com**

- Reknit is a business powered by lifelong knitters. Send them your old sweaters and for a fee they will unravel and clean the yarn and return a new scarf to you. **rekn.it**

To Read

The following books are excellent, eye-opening, and incredibly informative. You should be able to find copies of the books at your local library. *Preferred Fiber and Materials Market Report* and *The Paris Agreement* are available online for no charge.

- *American Cotton: Farm to Quilt*, Teresa Duryea Wong (Third Floor Quilts). This book is now out of print but you might be lucky enough to find a copy in your local library.

- *The Fabric of Civilization*, Virginia Postrel (Basic Books)

- *Fibershed*, Rebecca Burgess with Courtney White (Chelsea Green Publishing)

- *The Paris Agreement*, United Nations Framework Convention on Climate Change

- *Preferred Fiber and Materials Market Report*, Textile Exchange

- *Silent Spring*, Rachel Carson (Houghton Mifflin)

- *The Golden Thread*, Kassia St. Clair (Liveright)

To Watch

I have not been able to find movies specific to textile waste for the quilting industry but these movies discuss textiles as a whole, and I believe it's easy to substitute "quilting" for "fashion."

- *RiverBlue* documentary

- *Textile Mountain: The Hidden Burden of Our Fashion Waste*

- *The True Cost*

About the Author

Patty Murphy's passion for sewing began when she was a child, as she learned from her mother. She went on to create most of her wardrobe, and at age eighteen, Patty discovered quilt making with scraps from a pleated skirt disaster. She loves to work with bright, bold fabrics, exploring color by manipulating value in traditional designs.

Patty enjoys sharing her craft with others and has taught throughout the United States and around the world. Her work has been featured on magazine covers, in books, and on websites for major fabric manufacturers. Patty is the author of *Piecing Makeover* (by C&T Publishing) and the *Perfect Piecing Handy Pocket Guide* (by C&T Publishing).

When she isn't in her studio, Patty can be found cooking, baking, spending time with friends and family, and traveling. She lives in Marietta, Georgia, with her husband and two sons. Visit Patty online and follow on social media!

Website: pattymurphyhandmade.com

Facebook: /pattymurphyhandmade

Pinterest: /pattypmurphy

Instagram: @pattymurphyhandmade